GRANTS AND FUNDING

FEDERAL GRANT MANAGEMENT

GOVERNANCE AND FUNDING CHALLENGES

GRANTS AND FUNDING

Additional books in this series can be found on Nova's website under the Series tab.

Additional e-books in this series can be found on Nova's website under the e-books tab.

GRANTS AND FUNDING

FEDERAL GRANT MANAGEMENT

GOVERNANCE AND FUNDING CHALLENGES

VANESSA N. ROWLEY
EDITOR

Nova Science Publishers, Inc.
New York

For permission to use material from this book please contact us:
Telephone 631-231-7269; Fax 631-231-8175
Web Site: http://www.novapublishers.com

Library of Congress Cataloging-in-Publication Data

Rowley, Vanessa N.
Federal grant management : governance and funding challenges / editors, Vanessa N. Rowley.
p. cm.
Includes index.
ISBN 978-1-62100-185-0 (hardcover)
1. Grants-in-aid--United States--Management. I. Title.
HJ275.2.R68 2012
352.730973--dc23
2011031678

Published by Nova Science Publishers, Inc. † New York

CONTENTS

PREFACE

Grants play a significant role in implementing and funding federal programs. The federal government's use of grants to achieve national objectives and to respond to emerging trends, such as changing demographics and changing threats to homeland security, has grown significantly in the last two decades. While federal grant funding has been increasing, long-standing concerns remain about the federal government's grants management and the lack of effective oversight tools to reasonably assure that grants are used for their intended purposes and that risks of fraud, waste and abuse are minimized. This book presents the grant management process as well as ways to improve oversight and accountability of federal grants.

Chapter 1- While federal grant funding has been increasing, long-standing concerns remain about the federal government's grants management and the lack of effective oversight tools to reasonably assure that grants are used for their intended purposes and that risks of fraud, waste, and abuse are minimized. GAO has issued a range of reports raising concerns about the risks and vulnerabilities related to grants management and oversight. The Administration recognizes these concerns. It included improving grants management as a part of its initiative to eliminate waste in the U.S. government and has various efforts underway to improve grants oversight and accountability.

Chapter 2- Grants management has long been a challenge for the Department of Justice (Department or DOJ). The Department has three major grant-awarding agencies, the Office of Justice Programs (OJP), Office on Violence Against Women (OVW), and the Office of Community Oriented Policing Services (COPS). These agencies provide grants to state, local, tribal, and private organizations to conduct research, support law enforcement activities, provide training and technical assistance, and implement criminal justice-related programs.

Chapter 3- Federal grant-in-aid programs, also commonly referred to as "federal grant programs" or "federal domestic assistance programs," transfer money, property, services, or other items of value to assist eligible recipients accomplish purposes authorized by Congress. For the purposes of my testimony today, federal grant programs include entitlement grants, formula grants, and discretionary grants. Entitlement grants provide funding for grantees who meet specific statutory requirements. Formula grants use allocation formulas established in statute to award funds. Discretionary grants are awarded through a competitive process administered by the federal grantor agencies. My testimony will include general observations concerning agency activities in the administration of federal grants. Specifically, I will discuss challenges to transparency in the pre-award phase of grants administration and whether the level of agency discretion influences the need for transparency.

Chapter 4- The Federal Government has a fundamental responsibility to be an effective steward of taxpayers' money. This requires Federal agencies to implement rigorous financial management policies and controls to ensure that Federal funds are appropriately accounted for and wisely spent in accordance with laws and regulation. The Office of Management and Budget (OMB), working with Federal grant-making agencies and non-Federal stakeholders, has established policies and guidelines through OMB's grant management circulars and government–wide administrative common rules, codified by each grant-making agency. These policies and guidelines provide Federal agencies a solid framework to ensure that relevant program requirements are being met; that strong internal controls for reducing waste, fraud, and error are in place; and that grantees are meeting their responsibility for performance and accountability for the grant awards.

Chapter 5- Every year, hundreds of billions of taxpayer dollars are lost to waste, fraud, abuse and mismanagement. As an elected official, I take seriously my duty to safeguard taxpayers' investments in federal programs by ensuring their money is used effectively, efficiently and for sound purposes. This is for an important reason: when the government recklessly wastes taxpayer money, the public trust is undermined.

Chapter 6- In response to the Federal Financial Assistance Management Improvement Act of 1999, the Office of Management and Budget (OMB), among other things, deployed Grants.gov as the central grant identification and application portal for federal grant programs in 2003 and named the Department of Health and Human Services (HHS) its managing partner. As a result of funding and governance challenges— such as untimely contributions, a lack of performance metrics, unclear lines of authority, and confusion over roles and responsibilities among Grants.gov's governance bodies— that have adversely affected operations, GAO is required to examine (1) key factors HHS should consider when proposing a funding model for Grants.gov, and (2) how the Grants.gov governance bodies could address Grants.gov's previously identified governance challenges. To do this, GAO analyzed agency documents and interviewed officials at HHS, OMB, the Grants Executive Board (GEB), three case study agencies that manage similar E-Gov initiatives and three Grants.gov partner agencies.

Chapter 7- The Office of the Inspector General (OIG) Audit Division conducts internal audits of Department of Justice (D0J) granting agencies and external audits of grant recipients.[1] Internal audits assess overall grant program management in areas such as awarding grants, monitoring grantees, and assessing program performance and reporting. External audits assess a grantee's compliance with grant conditions, including budget management and control, drawdown and reimbursement requests, program income, subgrantee oversight, matching funds, financial reporting, and program reporting.

[1] Throughout this document, the term granting agencies refers to the Office of Justice Programs, the Office of Community Oriented Policing Services, and the Office on Violence Against Women.

In: Federal Grant Management
Editor: Vanessa N. Rowley
ISBN: 978-1-62100-185-0

Chapter 1

FEDERAL GRANTS: IMPROVEMENTS NEEDED IN OVERSIGHT AND ACCOUNTABILITY PROCESSES*

United States Government Accountability Office

Statement of Jeanette M. Franzel Managing Director
Financial Management and Assurance

WHY GAO DID THIS STUDY

While federal grant funding has been increasing, long-standing concerns remain about the federal government's grants management and the lack of effective oversight tools to reasonably assure that grants are used for their intended purposes and that risks of fraud, waste, and abuse are minimized. GAO has issued a range of reports raising concerns about the risks and vulnerabilities related to grants management and oversight. The Administration recognizes these concerns. It included improving grants management as a part of its initiative to eliminate waste in the U.S.

---

* This is an edited, reformatted and augmented version of the United States Government Accountability Office publication, Testimony Before the Subcommittee on Technology, Information Policy, Intergovernmental Relations and Procurement Reform, House of Representatives, dated June 23, 2011.

government and has various efforts underway to improve grants oversight and accountability.

This testimony addresses the (1) significance of federal grant funding, (2) risks and vulnerabilities in key controls in the federal grant life cycle, and (3) improvements needed to make the single audit process an effective accountability mechanism. This testimony is primarily based on prior GAO work that reviewed grant accountability and the single audit process.

What GAO Recommends

Through our body of work on federal grant accountability, GAO has made numerous recommendations directed at improving management and oversight. Our recommendations include a range of actions at the agency and governmentwide levels.

What GAO Found

Grants Play a Significant Role in Implementing and Funding Federal Programs. The federal government's use of grants to achieve national objectives and to respond to emerging trends, such as changing demographics and changing threats to homeland security, has grown significantly in the last two decades. From fiscal years 1990 to 2010, federal grant outlays to states and local governments, increased from about $135 billion to over $600 billion—almost one-fifth of the fiscal year 2010 federal budget, according to the Office of Management and Budget (OMB). In fiscal year 2010, over 1,670 federal grant programs were offered by 23 federal grant-making departments and agencies.

Risks and Vulnerabilities Exist in Key Controls in the Grant Life Cycle. Organizations that award and receive grants need effective internal control over the processes and funds involved. These controls are fundamental in assuring the proper and effective use of federal funds to achieve program goals and to ensure that funds are used for their intended purposes. Overall, our work on grant management has found weaknesses in the control systems of federal awarding agencies. We found vulnerabilities at different points in the grant life cycle: in the preaward, award, implementation, and closeout stages. Furthermore, we observed oversight issues that exist across the government.

For example, in 2008 we reported that in 2006 about $1 billion remained in undisbursed funding in expired grant accounts in the largest civilian grant payment system, which was associated with thousands of grantees and over 325 different federal programs and could have been identified through improved oversight and grant tracking. In addition, federal agencies reported an estimated $125.4 billion in improper payments for fiscal year 2010. This estimate was attributable to over 70 programs spread across 20 agencies. Many of those programs reporting improper payments were federal grant programs, including Medicaid.

Improvements Are Needed to Make Single Audits a More Effective Accountability Mechanism Over Grant Funding. The single audit process for organizations spending $500,000 or more in federal grant awards in a year is intended to play a key role in achieving accountability over federal grant resources. These audits report on the financial statements and internal controls over compliance with laws and grant provisions, among other things. GAO and others have identified and reported on significant concerns with the single audit process that diminish its effectiveness as an oversight accountability mechanism and concluded that improvements are needed. Through our work we found that (1) the federal oversight structure is not adequate to monitor the efficiency and effectiveness of the single audit process; (2) time frames of the single audit process do not facilitate the timely identification and correction of audit findings; and (3) single audit stakeholders have raised concerns about the complexity and relative costs and benefits of the single audit requirements, especially at smaller entities. Currently, OMB is conducting initiatives looking to improve the process, but time frames for implementing the results of ongoing studies are unclear.

Mr. Chairman,
Ranking Member Connolly, and
Other Members of the Subcommittee:

Thank you for the opportunity to be here today to discuss the issues that surround the federal grants management process and the need to improve grants management and oversight to help ensure accountability and the proper use of taxpayer dollars. While federal grant funding has been increasing, long-standing concerns remain about the federal government's grants management and the lack of effective oversight tools to reasonably assure that federal funds are used for their intended purposes and to minimize risks of fraud, waste, and abuse. Today I will highlight a range of reports we have issued that raise concerns about the risks and vulnerabilities related to the grants management and oversight process including the single audit process which is intended to be a key accountability mechanism.[1] The Administration also recognizes these concerns. It included improving grants management as part of its initiative to eliminate waste in the 2010 Financial Report of the U.S. Government and has various efforts underway intended to improve grants oversight and accountability.[2]

Today, I will discuss the (1) significance of federal grant funding, (2) risks and vulnerabilities in key controls in the federal grant life cycle, and (3) improvements needed to make the single audit process an effective accountability mechanism.

In preparing this testimony, we relied on our body of work on federal grants management and oversight, including the single audit process. More detail on our scope and methodology is included in each issued product. We conducted our work in June 2011 in accordance with all sections of GAO's Quality Assurance Framework that are relevant to our objectives.

The framework requires that we plan and perform the engagement to meet our stated objectives and that we discuss any limitations in our work. We believe that the information and data obtained, and the analysis conducted, provide a reasonable basis for our findings and conclusions.

GRANTS PLAY A SIGNIFICANT ROLE IN IMPLEMENTING AND FUNDING FEDERAL PROGRAMS

The federal government's use of grants to achieve national objectives and respond to emerging trends, such changing demographics and changing threats to homeland security, has grown significantly in the last two decades. According to the Office of Management and Budget (OMB), from fiscal years 1990 to 2010, federal outlays for grants to state and local governments increased from $135 billion to $608 billion—almost one-fifth of the federal budget and a 350 percent increase since fiscal year 1990 (see fig. 1).[3] In fiscal year 2010, OMB identified 23 federal grant–making departments and agencies that offered over 1,670 federal grant programs.[4] The top three agencies in terms of grant dollars outlayed during fiscal year 2010 were the Departments of Health and Human Services (HHS), Transportation, and Education.[5]

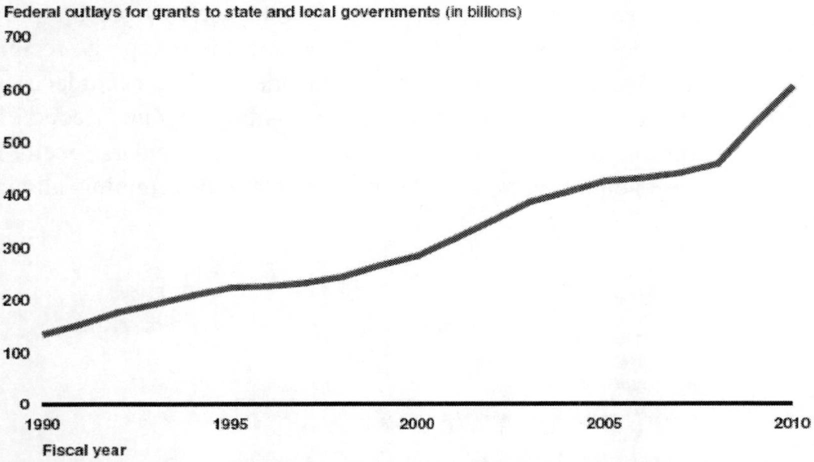

Source: Table 12.1 of the Historical Tables of the President's fiscal year 2012 budget, www.whitehouse.gov/omb/budget/Historicals.

Figure 1. Total Federal Outlays for Grants to State and Local Governments during Fiscal Years 1990 through 2010.

The Catalog of Federal Domestic Assistance (CFDA),[6] administered by the General Services Administration, provides information on grant programs within and across agencies. Our analysis of federal assistance data from the CFDA indicates that, as of June 17, 2011, 1,432 project grant programs and 209 formula grant programs were listed.[7] In addition, there were 34 grant programs that are categorized as a combination of both project and formula grants. The top three agencies in terms of number of grant programs on the CDFA Web site were the Departments of HHS, Interior, and Agriculture. The CFDA Web site allows users to search the database for grant programs on the basis of a range of factors, such as the awarding federal agency or the general nature of a grant program, such as health care or environmental quality. For example, our analysis identified 128 grant programs that address environmental quality issues.

Risks and Vulnerabilities Exist in Key Controls in the Grant Life Cycle

In awarding federal grants, effective oversight and internal control is of fundamental importance in assuring the proper and effective use of federal funds to achieve program goals. Effective internal control systems provide reasonable assurance to taxpayers that grants are awarded properly, recipients are eligible, and federal funds are used as intended and in accordance with applicable laws and regulations.[8] In authorizing grant programs, federal laws identify the types of activities that can be funded. OMB circulars specify how grants are to be administered and the standards for determining allowable costs.[9]

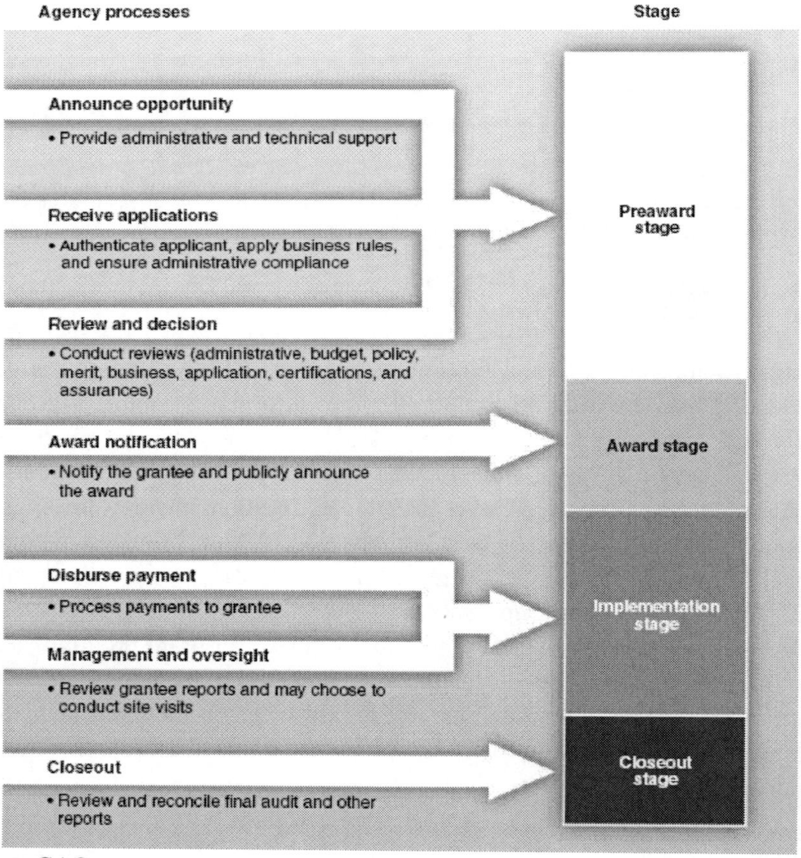

Source: GAO.

Figure 2. Grant Life Cycle of Federal Awarding Agency.

In addition to the legal and regulatory underpinnings, each grant program has stated purposes that guide what the grant is intended to accomplish. Before awarding any grants, agencies' preaward processes should ensure that potential recipients have the necessary capabilities to effectively implement the program to comply with relevant laws and regulations, and provide the necessary accountability for federal resources. Once the agency has awarded the grants, its monitoring of grantee performance is important to help ensure that grantees are meeting program and accountability requirements. Following grant completion, it is important for agencies to evaluate the goals and measures established at the beginning of the process against actual results, and to make any needed adjustments for future grant efforts. At all stages of the process, it is essential that effective internal control systems are in place. The grant life cycle is shown in figure 2.[10]

Overall our work on grant management and oversight issues found weaknesses in the control systems of the stages of the grant life cycle: the preaward and award stages, implementation, and close out.[11] We have recommended actions to strengthen the internal control framework for grant accountability in individual programs—including developing and implementing formal and structured approaches to conducting grant monitoring activities, and training grant program staff. While agencies have taken actions to address our recommendations in individual programs, more work is needed across the government as well as from a governmentwide perspective to strengthen internal controls and oversight for federal grant funds.

Key Controls in Agencies' Preaward and Award Processes Need Improvement

Our audits found that agencies awarded grants without adequately documenting the grantee selection process.[12] In some instances, we found agencies did not perform preaward reviews until after the grants had been awarded.[13] Preaward reviews are essential to determining that recipients possess, or have the ability to obtain, the necessary competence to plan and carry out the program before awarding a grant, thereby reducing the federal government's risk that money may be wasted or projects may not achieve intended results. For an effective preaward grant process, agencies need effective procedures for:

- assessing applicant capability to account for funds,
- competing grants in a fair and effective manner for grant programs that require competition,

- preparing good work plans to provide the framework for grant accountability, and
- including clear terms and conditions in award documents.

The award stage of grants management includes making award decisions and committing funds. In a competitive award process, agencies can increase assurance that recipients have the systems and resources to efficiently and effectively use funds to meet grant goals. Evaluation criteria, including having sufficient resources and sound management practices, can help an agency focus its review on factors indicative of success and provides information about grant applicants' ability to fulfill grant requirements.

We found weaknesses throughout the award processes used by agencies we reviewed. For example, in one review we found controls over the agency's processes had weaknesses in (1) carrying out and documenting management's review of grant applications, (2) documenting the grant award decisions, and (3) using the automated recipient data available in the agency's grants system. These deficiencies increased the risk that the agency would not consistently consider all relevant information— including key management discussions during evaluation—before making a decision to award. Lack of documentation also limited the agency's ability to explain the results of its award decisions, and resulted in incomplete and inaccurate information in the agency's grants and recipient-application evaluations. At the time of our review, the agency's grant-application evaluation process and the basis for the resulting decisions were not clearly documented.[14]

Another agency's decisions to award grants were based primarily on the results of a peer review process that had weak internal controls for ensuring that applications would be evaluated consistently. We found weaknesses in the procedures the agency relied on to ensure that evaluation criteria were applied consistently across reviewers and across panels when evaluating the grant applications it received.[15]

Weaknesses in the Implementation Stage Expose Funds to the Risk of Waste, Fraud, and Abuse

While federal grant-awarding agencies are responsible for continued oversight of the federal funds they award, grantees or recipients also have key responsibilities to administer, manage, and account for the use of grant funds. Federal agencies are dependent on the design and implementation of recipients' grant management programs to ensure that federal funds are used for their intended purposes and are appropriately safeguarded.

Over the past several years, we have reported that agencies need to improve oversight of grantee activities and management of federal funds.[16] Effective oversight procedures based on internal control standards for monitoring the recipients' use of awarded funds are key to ensuring that waste, fraud, and abuse are not overlooked and that program funds are being spent appropriately. Such procedures include (1) identifying the nature and extent of grant recipients' risks and managing those risks, (2) having skilled staff to oversee recipients to ensure they are using sound financial practices and meeting program objectives and requirements, and (3) using and sharing information about grant recipients throughout the organization. To ensure that grant funds are used for intended purposes, agencies need effective processes for:

- monitoring the financial management of grants,
- ensuring results through performance monitoring,
- using audits to provide valuable information about recipients, and
- monitoring subrecipients as a critical element of grant success.

We have also reported the need for agencies to assist recipients in improving subrecipient monitoring—the process of a recipient assessing its subrecipients' quality of performance over time and ensuring that the findings of audits and other reviews are promptly resolved. It is important that recipients identify, prioritize, and manage potential at-risk subrecipients to ensure that grant goals are reached and resources are used properly. Additionally, recipients should be (1) conducting site visits to subrecipients (early and often); (2) reviewing financial and progress reports for accuracy, completeness, and alignment with program objectives; and (3) and strengthening policies and procedures related to subrecipients. GAO has found that inadequate subrecipient monitoring often leads to the misuse, abuse, and waste of federal funds.

Grant Closeout Procedures Represent One of the Final Opportunities to Detect Unallowable Uses of Funds

Past audits of federal agencies by GAO and Inspectors General and annual performance reports by at least eight federal agencies in 2006 and 2007 suggest that grant management challenges, including grant closeout procedures, are a long-standing problem.[17] Closeout processes can be used for detecting problems that have occurred in areas such as recipient financial management and program operations, accounting for any real and personal property acquired with federal funds, making upward or downward adjustments to the federal share of costs, and receiving refunds that the recipient is not authorized to retain. Closeout procedures are intended to ensure that recipients have met all financial requirements, provided final reports, and returned any unused funds. When agencies do not conduct closeout procedures in a timely manner, this prevents unused funds from being used to help address the purpose of the grant and, at the same time, increases risk that records will be lost or officials may leave or not remember sufficient details, making it more difficult for the agency to recoup appropriate funds.

Attention Is Needed To Address Governmentwide Issues

Through our work, we found that weaknesses in grant oversight and accountability issues that span the government. Specifically, we identified long-standing challenges in oversight of undisbursed grant award balances, and significant levels of improper payments in grant programs.

Oversight of Undisbursed Balances in Federal Grant Programs

We have found that undisbursed balances for expired grant accounts can be significant and that agencies needed to improve how they track and report on these funds.[18] For example, in August 2008, we reported that during calendar year 2006 about $1 billion in undisbursed funding remained in expired grant accounts in the largest civilian grant payment system.[19] The expired but still open grant accounts found were associated with thousands of recipients and over 325 different federal programs. This figure illustrates the potential financial benefits to be gained by improving oversight of undisbursed grant funding, and we are currently starting follow-up work in this area. The existence of undisbursed grant balances in expired grant accounts may hinder the achievement of program objectives, limit deobligating funding for other uses, and expose the funding to improper spending or accounting.

Taken together, dozens of past audit reports we reviewed from multiple agencies suggested that undisbursed balances in expired grant accounts were a long-standing challenge and that these grants shared common grants management problems. The audits generally attributed the problems to inadequacies in the awarding agencies' grant management processes, including closeouts as a low management priority, inconsistent closeout procedures, poorly timed communications with grantees, or insufficient compliance or enforcement. Yet when agencies made concerted efforts to address the problem, Inspectors General and auditors reported that those agencies were able to improve the timeliness of grant closeouts and decrease the amount of undisbursed funding in expired grant accounts. The approaches taken by the agencies administering the grants generally focused on elevating timely grant closeouts to a higher agency management priority and on improving overall closeout processing.

Better tracking of grant accounts maintained in all federal payment systems could identify the expired grants with undisbursed balances and make funds available for other assistance projects or facilitate the return of these funds to the Treasury. We recommended in August 2008 that the Director of OMB instruct executive departments and independent agencies to annually track the amount of undisbursed grant funding remaining in expired grant accounts and report on the status and resolution of such funding in their annual performance plans and Performance and Accountability Reports. As of April 2011, OMB had not issued governmentwide guidance regarding undisbursed balances in expired grant accounts.[20]

Many Grant Programs Have Significant Levels of Improper Payments

Federal agencies reported improper payments of an estimated $125.4 billion in fiscal year 2010. This $125.4 billion estimate comes from over 70 programs spread among 20 federal agencies. Many of those programs reporting improper payments were federal grant programs. A majority of the $125.4 billion of reported improper payments is accounted for by 10 programs. The 10 programs account for about $118 billion, or 94 percent, of the total estimated improper payments reported for fiscal year 2010. Five of those top 10 programs were grant programs, and included improper payment estimates for Medicaid ($22.5 billion), Unemployment Insurance ($17.5 billion), Supplemental nutrition assistance programs ($2.2 billion), the National school lunch program ($1.5 billion), and Pell Grants ($1 billion).

Recently, in July 2010, the Improper Payments Elimination and Recovery Act (IPERA)[21] was enacted to enhance reporting and reduction of improper payments. In addition to amending the Improper Payments Information Act's improper payment estimation requirements, IPERA establishes additional requirements related to federal agency management accountability, recovery auditing, and compliance and noncompliance determinations and reporting. In addition, the Administration is taking a number of actions in the area of improper payments.

Establishing effective accountability measures to prevent and reduce improper payments in grant programs becomes an even higher priority in today's fiscal environment. In this regard, identifying and analyzing causes of improper payments will be key to developing effective corrective actions and accountability measures in order to reduce and prevent improper payments in grant programs.

IMPROVEMENTS ARE NEEDED TO MAKE SINGLE AUDITS A MORE EFFECTIVE ACCOUNTABILITY MECHANISM OVER FEDERAL GRANT FUNDING

OMB has indicated that single audits play a key role in the achievement of its accountability over federal grant funding. The Single Audit Act, as amended, was enacted to promote, among other things, sound financial management, including effective internal controls, with respect to federal grant awards administered by nonfederal entities. We and others have identified and reported on significant concerns with the Single Audit process that diminish its effectiveness as an oversight accountability mechanism and concluded that improvements are needed.[22] Accordingly, we have made several recommendations for improving the Single Audit process. In March 2009, we made recommendations to OMB for improving federal oversight and the single audit process.[23] In April 2009, we started work on American Recovery and Reinvestment Act of 2009 (Recovery Act) programs relating to single audits and issued the first of nine reports related to oversight and accountability mechanisms for Recovery Act funds.24 [25] We made additional recommendations for improving single audits during the course of that work. A summary of our findings and recommendations follows.

The Federal Oversight Structure Is Not Adequate to Monitor the Efficiency and Effectiveness of the Single Audit Process

We found that the federal oversight structure is not adequate to monitor the efficiency and effectiveness of the single audit process. Specifically, federal agencies do not systematically use audit findings to identify and understand emerging and persistent issues related to grant programs and grantee use of funds.[26] We identified variations in the federal oversight process in performing key functions of the single audit process such as quality control reviews by federal cognizant agencies which raised questions about how federal agencies carry out their single audit responsibilities. The federal oversight structure for the single audit process does not include a designated function or entity to monitor whether or how well federal awarding agencies are implementing single audit requirements. Without a mechanism in place to monitor on an ongoing basis how the single audit process is implemented governmentwide, OMB and federal stakeholders are unable to measure the efficiency and effectiveness of this process or its usefulness as an accountability tool over federal grant awards. We recommended that OMB designate an entity or group to (1) evaluate and comprehensively monitor the single audit process governmentwide, (2) assess the efficiency and effectiveness of how agencies carry out their single audit responsibilities, and (3) identify additional guidance and resources needed to carry out single audit requirements. OMB has developed workgroups which are currently underway to review ways to improve the single audit process. In June 2010, the Single Audit Workgroup established by OMB pursuant to Executive Order 13520 made recommendations to OMB in four areas to enhance and streamline the single audit process to better support the overall effort to improve federal program accountability and reduce improper payments.[27] However, as discussed in a later section, the related decisions and planning for acting on these recommendations are still in process. The four areas of recommendations included

1) instilling federal leadership over the single audit process to improve program accountability and reduce improper payments;
2) managing risks by refocusing the single audit to include those nonfederal entities that present the greatest risk of improper payments;
3) improving the access to information in single audit reports to enhance federal agency follow-up of audit findings and to coordinate single audit and improper payments analysis and results; and
4) amending the stated purposes of the Single Audit Act of 1984, as amended, to emphasize the importance of acting on single audit findings as a way to reduce the risk of improper payments.

More Timely Single Audit Reporting is Needed, Especially in Internal Control

Time frames of the single audit process do not facilitate the timely identification and correction of audit findings.[28] [29] Under the current time frames for identifying and correcting audit findings provided by the Single Audit Act and OMB Circular No. A-133, it could take years to correct significant deficiencies and material weaknesses that expose federal funds to misuse or fraud. For example, in accordance with current requirements, a material weakness that has been identified by the auditor for an entity that has a June 30, 2010, fiscal year-end can possibly be reported in the Single Audit report to be issued as late as March 31, 2011, along with the auditee's corrective action plan. The federal awarding agency would have 6 months or until September 30, 2011, from receipt of the Single Audit report to communicate a written management decision to the auditee. As a result, it may take 15 months or more since the end of the fiscal year in which the audit finding was initially identified before an auditee's corrective action plan is approved by the federal agency.

Several state auditors have expressed frustration regarding single audit findings that remain open years after they were initially identified, without the auditee or the federal awarding agency taking action. The lack of attention to ensuring prompt corrective action impairs the federal government's ability to ensure that unallowable costs have been repaid or that internal control deficiencies have been corrected. Shortening the time frames required for issuing management decisions by federal agencies, and monitoring the auditee's implementation of timely corrective actions by the federal agency would help to ensure that appropriate audit follow-up and resolution are achieved, and that known internal control weaknesses are corrected.

In our work on Recovery Act funds, we reported our concern that the single audit process would not provide the timely accountability and focus needed to assist recipients in making necessary adjustments to internal controls to provide assurances that the Recovery Act funding was being spent as effectively as possible to meet program objectives. We also reported that the Single Audit reporting deadline is too late to provide audit results in time for the audited entity to take action on internal control deficiencies noted in Recovery Act programs.

In response to several of our recommendations, in October 2009 OMB implemented the Single Audit Internal Control project to encourage earlier reporting and timely correction of internal control deficiencies identified in single audits that included Recovery Act programs. Although we found that the project met its original objectives of (1) achieving more than 10 volunteer states participating in the project, (2) having the participating auditors issue interim internal control reports for the selected programs at least 3 months earlier, and (3) having auditee management issue corrective action plans to resolve internal control deficiencies at least 2 months earlier than required by OMB Circular No. A-133, the coverage of the project was limited, with 16 of the 50 states participating. Furthermore, because most of the federal awarding agencies did not issue their management decisions in a timely manner, grant recipients were delayed in implementing corrective action plans.

We also identified concerns regarding the need for OMB to issue its annual single audit guidance in a more timely manner. While OMB has committed to issuing its guidance in a timely manner, it has yet to achieve its target for issuance of its guidance. Specifically for 2009, OMB issued the guidance, Circular No. A-133 Compliance Supplement, in two stages, the initial one in May 2009 and an addendum in August 2009, after the single audits for entities with a June 30, 2009, fiscal year end were already under way.[30] An OMB official told us the delays in issuing the 2009 compliance supplement were due to incorporating more specific guidance for Recovery Act programs. For most of the largest nonfederal entities that are subject to the single audit, the fiscal year ends on June 30 and thus the timing of OMB's issuance of the audit guidance has been close to and even after the fiscal year end close. Most of the auditors told us that they needed the information as early as February or at least by April to effectively plan their work for a June 30 year end audit. Some of these auditors stated that the OMB guidance was issued too late, causing inefficiencies and disruptions in the planning of audit procedures. For 2010, OMB officials told us that they planned to issue the 2010 Compliance Supplement in late May 2010. However, the guidance was not issued until July 29, 2010. We recommended that OMB issue the guidance by March 31st of each year. In January 2011, OMB officials reported that the production of the 2011 Compliance Supplement was on schedule for issuance by March 31, 2011; however, OMB issued the 2011 Compliance Supplement on June 1, 2011. The late guidance impacts the auditors' ability to deliver timely results in what is already a lengthy process.

Need to Focus on High-Risk Activities, Programs, and Recipients while Potentially Streamlining, Simplifying, or Reducing Focus on Areas of Low Risk

Single audit stakeholders have raised concerns about the complexity and relative costs and benefits of the audit requirements for single audits, especially at the smaller entities.[31] Specifically, auditors of single audits are subject to similar audit requirements and the same guidance in OMB Circular No. A-133 and the Compliance Supplement when they are auditing an entity that has expended $500,000 of federal awards as they are when auditing one that expended $50 million or more. We found that there are opportunities to evaluate the audit procedures being applied and determine whether there is a proper balance between risk and cost-effective accountability from the largest to the smallest of audited entities. Single audits of small entities could be simplified while still meeting the accountability objectives of the Single Audit Act. For audits of large entities, opportunities could be explored to identify best practices and provide guidance for achieving higher-quality single audits. Our analysis shows significant disparities in the number of audits of small entities versus the number of audits of large entities and their respective coverage of federal award expenditures. The current one-size-fits-all approach to single audits, combined with the fact that less than 3 percent of audits cover about 85 percent of federal award expenditures subject to a single audit, presents a convincing case for reexamining the overall approach for performing single audits.[32] Because action had not been taken to address concerns about complexity and the need for streamlining, we further recommended during our Recovery Act work that OMB evaluate options for providing relief related to audit requirements for low-risk programs to balance new audit responsibilities associated with the Recovery Act.

OMB Has Implemented Some Recommendations but More Work Is Needed

OMB has taken initiative and is conducting studies to improve the Single Audit process but time frames for implementing the results of these studies are unclear. OMB officials have created a workgroup that combines two previous workgroups: the Executive Order 13520 – Reducing Improper Payments Section 4 (b) Single Audit Recommendations Workgroup (Single Audit

Workgroup), and the Circular No. A-87 - Cost Principles for State, Local, and Indian Tribal Governments Workgroup (Circular No. A-87 Workgroup).

The Single Audit Workgroup comprises representatives from the federal audit community; federal agency management officials involved in overseeing the single audit process and programs subject to that process; representatives from the state audit community; and staff from OMB. OMB officials tasked the Single Audit Workgroup with developing recommendations for improving the effectiveness of single audits of nonfederal entities that expend federal funds to help identify and reduce improper payments. In June 2010, the Single Audit Workgroup developed recommendations, some of which are targeted towards providing relief to auditors who audit recipients and grants under the requirements of the Single Audit Act. OMB officials stated that the recommendations warrant further study and that the workgroup is continuing its work on the recommendations. OMB officials also stated that the Circular No. A-87 Workgroup has also made recommendations that could impact single audits and that the two workgroups have been collaborating to ensure that the recommendations related to single audit improvements are compatible and could improve the single audit process. The combined workgroups plan to issue a report to OMB by August 29, 2011. We will continue to monitor OMB's progress to achieve this objective.

CONCLUSIONS

With the growth of federal grant funding over the past two decades, the increasing role of grants in achieving national objectives, and constrained resources available to meet diverse needs, attention to improving grants management and oversight can help ensure that resources are targeted to the intended recipients and are used effectively. Because many national objectives are now being carried out through state, local, and nongovernmental organizations, enhancing accountability and oversight at all levels is equally important, and these efforts should be mindful of the scarce oversight and accountability resources and shared responsibilities as improvements are made. Also, the long-standing problems that impeded the effectiveness of the single audit process as a key accountability mechanism for ensuring that federal grant funds are spent appropriately need to be addressed. Looking across the federal grants management and oversight processes, there is great potential for streamlining and simplifying while at the same time, improving accountability for how our federal dollars are spent by addressing the issues and weaknesses we have identified. We have been working with OMB to identify specific actions that could help streamline administrative processes and provide more flexibility for states in the audit and cost allocation process. We stand ready to assist the Subcommittee as it focuses attention on addressing these important issues, and to work constructively with OMB and the agencies.

Mr. Chairman, this concludes my statement. I will be happy to answer any questions you or the Subcommittee Members may have.

End Notes

[1] The Single Audit Act requires states, local governments, and nonprofit organizations expending $500,000 or more in federal awards in a year to obtain an audit in accordance with the requirements set forth in the act. A single audit consists of (1) an audit and opinions on the fair presentation of the financial statements and the Schedule of Expenditures of Federal Awards; (2) gaining an understanding of and testing internal control over financial reporting and the entity's compliance with laws, regulations, and contract or grant provisions that have a direct and material effect on certain federal programs (i.e., the program requirements); and (3) an audit and an opinion on compliance with applicable program requirements for certain federal programs.

[2] U.S. Department of the Treasury, management's discussion and analysis section of the *2010 Financial Report of the United States Government,* (Washington, D.C.: December 2010).

[3] These amounts include Medicaid. According to OMB budgetary guidance and Pub. L. No. 107-300, Medicaid is the largest dollar federal grant program. See OMB Circular A-133 Compliance Supplement 2011.

[4] The 23 listed agencies included a category for "all other agencies."

[5] Outlay is the issuance of checks, disbursement of cash, or electronic transfer of funds made to liquidate a federal obligation. Outlays also occur when interest on Treasury debt held by the public accrues and when the government issues bonds, notes, debentures, monetary credits, or other cash-equivalent instruments in order to liquidate obligations.

[6] The *Catalog of Federal Domestic Assistance* (CFDA) is the single authoritative, governmentwide compendium and source document for descriptions of federal programs that provide assistance or benefits to the American public. The CFDA data are available on the Web at www.CFDA.gov.

[7] Formula grants allocate funds based on distribution formulas prescribed by legislation or administrative regulation.

[8] A Domestic Working Group, *Guide to Opportunities for Improving Grant Accountability* (Oct. 2005), available at http://www.ignet.gov/randp/rpts1.html.

[9] Such circulars include OMB Circular A-102, *Grants and Cooperative Agreements With State and Local Governments* (Oct. 7, 1994; further amended Aug. 29, 1997), and OMB Circular A-133, *Audits of States, Local Governments and Non-Profit Organizations* (includes revisions published in the *Federal Register* on June 27, 2003, and June 26, 2007).

[10] GAO, *Grants Management: Enhancing Performance Accountability Provisions Could Lead to Better Results*, GAO-06-1046 (Washington, D.C.; Sept. 29, 2006).

[11] Despite substantial variation among grants, grants generally follow a similar life cycle and include the preaward stage—potential recipients submit applications for agency review; the award stage—the agency identifies successful applicants or legislatively defined grant recipients and awards funding; the implementation stage—includes payment processing, agency monitoring, and recipient reporting, which may include financial and performance information; and the closeout phase—includes the preparation of final reports, financial reconciliation, and any required accounting for property.

[12] GAO, *Surface Transportation: Competitive Grant Programs Could Benefit from Increased Performance Focus and Better Documentation of Key Decisions*, GAO-11-234 (Washington, D.C.: Mar. 30, 2011), and *Intercity Passenger Rail: Recording Clearer Reasons for Awards Decisions Would Improve Otherwise Good Grantmaking Practices*, GAO-11-283, (Washington, D.C.: Mar. 10, 2011).

[13] GAO, *Foreign Assistance: U.S. Democracy Assistance for Cuba Needs Better Management and Oversight*, GAO-07-147 (Washington, D.C.: Nov. 15, 2006).

[14] GAO, *Legal Services Corporation: Improvements Needed in Controls over Grant Awards and Grantee Program Effectiveness*, GAO-10-540 (Washington, D.C.: June 11, 2010).

[15] GAO, *Runaway and* Homeless *Youth Grants*: *Improvements Needed in the Grant Award Process,* GAO-10-335 (Washington, D.C.: May 10, 2010).

[16] GAO, *Legal Services Corporation: Improved Internal Controls Needed in Grants Management and Oversight*, GAO-08-37 (Washington, D.C.: Dec. 28, 2007), and GAO, *Grant Monitoring: Department of Education Could Improve Its Processes with Greater Focus on Assessing Risks, Acquiring Financial Skills, and Sharing Information*, GAO-10-57 (Washington, D.C.: Nov. 19, 2009).

[17] GAO, *Grants Management: Attention Needed to Address Undisbursed Balances in Expired Grant Accounts.* GAO-08-432 (Washington, D.C.: Aug. 29, 2008); GAO, *University Research: Policies for the Reimbursement of Indirect Costs Need to Be Updated.* GAO-10-937 (Washington, D.C.: Sept. 8, 2010); *Youthbuild Program: Analysis of Outcome Data Needed to Determine Long-Term Benefits.* GAO-07-82 (Washington, D.C.: Feb. 28, 2007).

[18] GAO, *Grants Management: Attention Needed to Address Undisbursed Balances in Expired Grant Accounts.* GAO-08-432 (Washington, D.C.: Aug. 29, 2008).

[19] In 2006, the system made grant payments for nine federal departments and three other federal entities, accounting for about 70 percent of all federal grant disbursements.

[20] GAO, *Managing for Results: GPRA Modernization Act Implementation Provides Important Opportunities to Address Government Challenges*, GAO-11-617T (Washington, D.C.: May 10, 2011).

[21] Pub.L.No. 111-204, 124 Stat. 2224 (July 22, 2010).

[22] The President's Council on Integrity and Efficiency (PCIE) issued its *Report on National Single Audit Sampling Project*4 in June 2007, which raised significant concerns about the quality of single audits and made recommendations aimed at improving the quality of those audits.

[23] GAO, *Single Audit: Opportunities Exist to Improve the Single Audit Process and Oversight*, GAO-09-307R (Washington, D.C.: Mar. 13, 2009).

[24] GAO, *Recovery Act: As Initial Implementation Unfolds in States and Localities, Continued Attention to Accountability Issues Is Essential,* GAO-09-580 (Washington, D.C. Apr. 23, 2009)

[25] Pub. L. No. 111-5, 123 Stat. 115 (February 17, 2009).

[26] GAO, *Single Audit: Opportunities Exist to Improve the Single Audit Process and Oversight*, GAO-09-307R (Washington, D.C.: Mar. 13, 2009).

[27] *Executive Order 13520 – Reducing Improper Payments Section 4 (b) Single Audit Workgroup Recommendations, June 4, 2010.*

[28] The Single Audit Act requires that recipients submit their financial reporting packages, including the Single Audit report, to the federal government's audit clearinghouse 30 days after receipt of the auditor's report or within 9 months after the end of the period being audited, whichever comes first. As a result, an audited entity may not receive feedback needed to correct an identified internal control deficiency over compliance until the latter part of the subsequent fiscal year.

[29] GAO, *Recovery Act: Opportunities To Improve Management And Strengthen Accountability Over States' And Localities' Uses Of Funds*, GAO-10-999 (Washington, D.C. Sept. 20, 2010).

[30] The compliance supplement is issued annually to guide auditors on what program requirements should be tested for programs audited as part of the single audit and has been the primary mechanism that OMB has used to provide Recovery Act requirements to auditors.

[31] GAO, *Single Audit: Opportunities Exist to Improve the Single Audit Process and Oversight*, GAO-09-307R (Washington, D.C.: Mar. 13, 2009).

[32] GAO, *Single Audit: Opportunities Exist to Improve the Single Audit Process and Oversight*, GAO-09-307R (Washington, D.C.: Mar. 13, 2009).

In: Federal Grant Management
Editor: Vanessa N. Rowley
ISBN: 978-1-62100-185-0

Chapter 2

STATEMENT OF CYNTHIA A. SCHNEDAR ACTING INSPECTOR GENERAL, U.S. DEPARTMENT OF JUSTICE, BEFORE THE U.S. HOUSE OF REPRESENTATIVES COMMITTEE ON OVERSIGHT AND GOVERNMENT REFORM, SUBCOMMITTEE ON TECHNOLOGY, INFORMATION POLICY, INTERGOVERNMENTAL RELATIONS AND PROCUREMENT REFORM ON "IMPROVING OVERSIGHT AND ACCOUNTABILITY IN FEDERAL GRANT PROGRAMS"*

Mr. Chairman, Congressman Connolly, and Members of the Subcommittee:

Thank you for inviting me to testify about improving oversight and accountability in federal grant programs.

---

* This is an edited, reformatted and augmented version of testimony given by Cynthia A. Schnedar, Acting Inspector General, U.S. Department of Justice before the House Committee on Oversight and Government Reform on June 23, 2011.

Grants management has long been a challenge for the Department of Justice (Department or DOJ). The Department has three major grant-awarding agencies, the Office of Justice Programs (OJP), Office on Violence Against Women (OVW), and the Office of Community Oriented Policing Services (COPS). These agencies provide grants to state, local, tribal, and private organizations to conduct research, support law enforcement activities, provide training and technical assistance, and implement criminal justice-related programs.

Beginning in 2009, the Department faced heightened challenges in grant management because it had to award $4 billion in grants under the *American Recovery and Reinvestment Act of 2009* (Recovery Act) Act at the same time that it had to award the $3 billion in grant funding contained in the Department's annual FY 2009 appropriations. In addition, the Department received over $4 billion in FY 2010 grant funds to award, and another $4 billion in 2011. Through May 2011, the Department has obligated more than 99 percent of its Recovery Act funds and the grantees have received approximately 67 percent of the Recovery Act funds that have been obligated.

Given the large volume of grant funding traditionally awarded by the Department, the Department of Justice Office of the Inspector General (DOJ-OIG) has long focused its attention on overseeing the Department's efforts at grants management. We have conducted numerous audits and investigated a variety of fraud allegations involving Department grant funds. In FY 2010 we issued more than 60 audit reports of the Department's management of various grant programs and of the grant recipients and other agencies that conduct business with the Department. In addition, since 2009, we have initiated 63 grant fraud investigations, 16 of which relate to Recovery Act cases.

In my remarks this morning, I will first discuss some of the significant improvements that the Department has made in recent years in improving its grants management process. I will then discuss the challenges that we have identified that the Department faces in awarding grants and in providing adequate oversight after grant funds are awarded. I will then review the DOJ-OIG's efforts to provide training and other assistance to the government and Department in an effort to enhance the government's grants management capabilities.

THE DEPARTMENT'S RECENT IMPROVEMENTS TO ITS GRANTS MANAGEMENT PRACTICES

We have found that the Department has made a concerted effort in recent years to improve its regular grant management practices. In 2009, shortly after the passage of the Recovery Act, the OIG developed a document, entitled *Improving the Grants Management Process* (http://www.justice.gov/oig /special/s0903/final.pdf), which contains a series of recommendations and best practices in grant management that federal agencies should consider implementing. The Department responded positively to the recommendations in this document and has implemented changes in its grant management practices, including expanding the use of online training opportunities among grant recipients and assisting grantees in determining the appropriate performance information to collect.

In March 2011, we released a report examining the Department's efforts for monitoring and overseeing Recovery Act and non-Recovery Act grants awarded through its OJP. Our report found that OJP had made significant improvements in its monitoring and oversight of grants, primarily due to the establishment of its Office of Audit, Assessment and Management (OAAM).

OAAM was created in January 2006 to conduct and coordinate program assessments of grants awarded by OJP and COPS. Our audit found that initially after OAAM's creation, OJP made slow progress in staffing OAAM and in ensuring that OAAM's monitoring efforts were effective. In an assessment we made in 2008, two years after the passage of the statute creating OAAM, we found that OJP had not devoted sufficient effort to ensuring that OAAM was adequately staffed to oversee and monitor OJP grants, despite the congressional directive and the importance of OAAM's mission.

However, our March 2011 audit found that since January 2008, OAAM has made significant progress. Although OJP did not hire a permanent OAAM director until January 2009, OAAM had filled its allotted positions as of May 2009 with 49 federal and contractor positions. We found that OJP and OAAM have developed a reasonable process for providing monitoring to a high volume of grants, which have allowed them to monitor grants totaling almost four times the award amount required to be monitored by law. Other improvements included the establishment of a working group to review existing monitoring practices and develop standard monitoring approaches and procedures; the use of grant tools such as the Grants Management System,

Grant Monitoring Tool, and the Grant Assessment Tool; updates to the Grant Manager's Manual; and revisions to site visit documentation and the quality of site visit reports.

Despite OJP's improvements in monitoring and oversight of grants, we found that the OVW and COPS perform certain monitoring and oversight services that are duplicative of the services available through OJP. To eliminate such duplication and provide uniformity in oversight among Department granting agencies, we recommended that the Department should standardize the oversight services provided to the OVW and COPS.

CHALLENGES FACING THE DEPARTMENT IN GRANTS MANAGEMENT

While we believe the Department has taken positive steps toward improving its grants management practices, these changes will take time to fully implement and to incorporate into the Department's regular practices. As a result, the DOJ-OIG has continued to include grants management in its annual list of Top Management and Performance Challenges for the Department of Justice. Our work has continued to identify areas where the Department could further improve its management of grants, particularly in terms of the Department's processes for awarding grants and its oversight of grantees' internal controls.

Department's Process of Awarding Grants

Overall, the DOJ-OIG has found that the Department has strived to conduct the grant awarding process in a timely and fair manner, and in recent years, it has implemented policies to enhance transparency. However, our audits found that the Department's program offices and bureaus did not always assess the programmatic, financial, and administrative areas of the grants before making awards, and they also did not retain adequate documentation to support their review work. Therefore, we believe that the Department still needs to make improvements in the following areas:

(i) ranking of grant applications;
(ii) consistent treatment of applicants;
(iii) documentation and justification of award decisions; and
(iv) procedures to reduce the risk of conflicts of interest in the awarding process.

Ranking Applications. Some of our reviews have found that the Department should implement better controls to ensure that it correctly scores grant applications. For example, in May 2010, we issued an audit report on the selection process for the $1 billion COPS Hiring Recovery Program, which awards grants to state and local entities for the hiring, rehiring, and retention of career law enforcement officers. Our audit determined that COPS used inaccurate formulas in developing the scores and ranks of applicants, which resulted in the allocation of grants to 45 entities that should not have received grants, while another 34 entities that should have received grants did not. In response to our audit, COPS informed us that it has corrected the formulas for future use and modified its FY 2010 hiring grant allocation process.

We found a similar calculation error in our July 2010 audit of the OVW administration of $225 million in grant funding, where we found several instances where OVW internal peer reviewers incorrectly tabulated individual application scores and thus incorrectly ranked some applications higher than others. The OVW concurred with our recommendation to implement better internal controls that will check for scoring errors and verify the accuracy of future final peer review scores.

Consistent Treatment of Applicants. Our reviews have found instances where the Department was not treating grant applications in a consistent manner. For example, we found instances where the Department allowed some grant applications to continue through the competitive process for a grant award even though they were missing key documentation, while denying other applicants further consideration for the same deficiencies. We also found differences in the processes OJP's Bureau of Justice Assistance (BJA) and its Office of Juvenile Justice and Delinquency Prevention (OJJDP) used for computing final scores for applications. Having OJP bureaus and program offices use different methodologies for calculating peer review scores for similar Recovery Act programs may raise an appearance of inequitable treatment of applicants. As a result of the audit, OJP issued guidance to its bureaus and program offices implementing a standard approach with respect to normalization of peer review scoring.

Documentation of Award Decisions. Our recent audits also found some Department agencies do not consistently document the rationale for discretionary awards, and in some instances, do not explain why some applications ranked lower by peer reviewers received grants over higher-ranked applications. Although the Department is not required to award grants based solely on peer reviewer rankings, we believe that it should document the rationale for award decisions that deviate from peer review results.

Conflicts of Interest. Our recent audits reported concerns regarding procedures used to mitigate the risk of conflicts of interest in the award selection process. For example, our July 2010 audit of the OVW revealed in at least 23 instances, peer reviewers signed forms indicating they had no conflict of interest with the grant applicants before the peer reviewers knew who the grant applicants were that they would be reviewing.

In addition, our February 2011 audit of the BJA's Recovery Act Correctional Facilities on Tribal Lands Grant Program revealed that an internal BJA peer reviewer had significant involvement with an applicant that received an award. Specifically, the peer reviewer had participated in the applicant's Advisory Committee, but still certified that he had no conflicts of interest while reviewing program applications. As a result of these issues, the OJP and OVW agreed to implement corrections to strengthen conflict of interest procedures.

Department's Oversight of Grantees to Ensure Proper Internal Controls

In addition, our audits of individual grantees have found deficiencies in the grantees' use of grant awards. For example, in August 2010, we reported on our individual audits of 12 Byrne Justice Assistance Grant (JAG) grantees. In that report, we identified the following deficiencies among some of the grantees: (1) not segregating duties over payroll functions; (2) not employing sufficient staff with the training and experience to properly manage the grants; (3) not placing equipment items purchased with grant funds into operation until years after purchase; (4) not maintaining property disposal records; (5) not having sufficient staff to adequately manage and oversee subrecipients of Byrne JAG funds; and (6) not submitting timely and accurate financial, progress, and Recovery Act reports. Based on these grantee audit results, we recommended that the Office of Justice Programs provide additional training and oversight. As of June 2011, corrective action was still in progress.

Outstanding Recommendations to the Department

We also believe that the Department can take further action to address outstanding recommendations to resolve questioned costs from our audits of grantees. Every year we issue hundreds of audit recommendations to the Department's grant-awarding components to help enhance grants management and ensure the remedy of mismanaged and unsupported grant funds. For example, in FY 2010, we issued over 300 internal and external audit recommendations to OJP, COPS, and the OVW. Frequently, the agencies are able to implement the recommendations within a year or two. However, in some instances the Department takes several years to implement an audit recommendation. For example, grant audit recommendations we issued in 1999 for OJP to remedy over $160,000 in questioned costs remain open. In addition, grant audit recommendations we made in 2003 will remain open until COPS remedies almost $1 million in questioned costs and provides documentation that a key grant requirement was fulfilled.

In addition, we released an audit report in 2006 on the Department's grant closeout process in which we recommended that OVW resolve $37 million in questioned costs related to grant drawdowns occurring more than 90 days past the grant end date and de-obligate and put to better use over $14 million obligated to expired grants that were already 90 days past the grant end date in 2006. We have had multiple communications with OVW about these issues since we issued our report in 2006, but OVW has yet to fully resolve these recommendations.

DOJ-OIG Initiatives to Enhance Grants Management Capabilities

We recognize that Inspectors General also play an important role in improving oversight and accountability in federal grant programs. In light of this, the DOJ OIG has a multidisciplinary effort to provide advice to the DOJ grant-awarding components, train grant managers on fraud risks, proactively reach out to state and local agencies receiving funding from DOJ, perform audits and evaluations of the DOJ's use of funding, and perform any necessary investigative activity.

We also have been an active participant in the grant fraud efforts of the inter-agency National Procurement Fraud Task Force (NPFTF) since its inception, and it has now been consolidated into the Recovery Act,

Procurement and Grant Fraud Working Group of the President's Financial Fraud Enforcement Task Force (FFETF). In 2009, as the Chair of the Grant Fraud Committee of the NPFTF, the DOJ-OIG published a document entitled, "*A Guide to Grant Oversight and Best Practices for Combating Grant Fraud*" (which can be found at: http://www.justice.gov/oig/special/s0902a/index.htm). This document was developed with several other Departments' input and presents broad recommendations for enhancing grant oversight.

Currently, the Grant Fraud Committee, which I chair, is working on several training and outreach initiatives, including developing an interactive online grant fraud training program for grantees regarding grant management and a video training program for federal attorneys regarding both criminal and civil enforcement tools that can be used to combat grant fraud. The Grant Fraud Committee also played a key role in developing the grant fraud training course for agents and auditors that has been offered for the past three years at the Federal Law Enforcement Training Center (FLETC).

In addition, the DOJ-OIG has provided extensive training on prevention and deterrence of grant fraud to DOJ grant recipients. Since the enactment of the Recovery Act in February 2009, the DOJ-OIG has trained more than 5,800 federal, state, and local program managers and participants on Recovery Act fraud awareness and conducted 105 outreach sessions with state and local agencies. We also are continuing with our extensive auditing of DOJ grants and with our vigorous investigations of any allegations of fraud in DOJ grant programs.

CONCLUSION

We will continue to work with Department components and external agencies to help reduce risks associated with federal grants. We believe the Department is demonstrating a commitment to improving its grants management process, and we have seen significant signs of improvement in this area. However, further improvements are needed, and considerable work remains before managing the billions of dollars the Department awards annually in grants is no longer a top challenge for the Department.

This concludes my prepared statement, and I would be pleased to answer any questions.

In: Federal Grant Management
Editor: Vanessa N. Rowley
ISBN: 978-1-62100-185-0

Chapter 3

TESTIMONY OF NATALIE M. KEEGAN ANALYST IN AMERICAN FEDERALISM AND EMERGENCY MANAGEMENT POLICY, CONGRESSIONAL RESEARCH SERVICE BEFORE THE HOUSE SUBCOMMITTEE ON TECHNOLOGY, INFORMATION POLICY, INTERGOVERNMENTAL RELATIONS, AND PROCUREMENT REFORM*

Good morning Chairman Lankford, Ranking Member Connolly, and members of the Committee. My name is Natalie Keegan and I am an analyst in American federalism and emergency management policy with the Congressional Research Service. Thank you for the opportunity to testify this morning on improving oversight and accountability in federal grant programs.

Federal grant-in-aid programs, also commonly referred to as "federal grant programs" or "federal domestic assistance programs," transfer money, property, services, or other items of value to assist eligible recipients accomplish purposes authorized by Congress. For the purposes of my

* This is an edited, reformatted and augmented version of testimony given by Natalie M. Keegan Analyst in American Federalism and Emergency Management Policy, Congressional Research Service Before the House Subcommittee on Technology, Information Policy, Intergovernmental Relations, and Procurement Reform on June 23, 2011.

testimony today, federal grant programs include entitlement grants, formula grants, and discretionary grants. Entitlement grants provide funding for grantees who meet specific statutory requirements. Formula grants use allocation formulas established in statute to award funds. Discretionary grants are awarded through a competitive process administered by the federal grantor agencies. My testimony will include general observations concerning agency activities in the administration of federal grants. Specifically, I will discuss challenges to transparency in the pre-award phase of grants administration and whether the level of agency discretion influences the need for transparency.

CONGRESSIONAL OVERSIGHT OF FEDERAL GRANTS

Congress often pursues oversight of federal grants through the authorization and appropriations processes, and through investigative oversight to gather information on the administration and effectiveness of a federal grant program. Congress also exercises oversight through the federal grant application process. It is useful to view Congressional oversight of grants in two overarching phases; pre-award and post-award.

Pre-award oversight activities may include grant program authorizations and appropriations, determinations of eligibility and eligible activities, review of announcements of funding availability, and review of panel scorings of eligible applications. Post-award oversight activities may include audits, reporting requirements, and prevention and investigation of waste, fraud, and abuse.

While recent Congressional debate has involved post-award activities, particularly recipient and agency reporting requirements, consideration of congressional oversight of pre-award activities may provide insight into improving oversight and accountability in federal grants.

PRE-AWARD OVERSIGHT OF FEDERAL GRANTS

Congressional authorization of federal grant programs began in 1862 with the authorization of The Morrill Land Grant Act of July 2, 1862, to establish land-grant colleges.[1] Since that time, there has been dramatic growth in federal assistance programs.[2] Currently, there are 2,123 congressionally authorized federal domestic assistance programs.[3] Five federal agencies administer 1,165 of these programs. Federal outlays for grants to state and local governments have grown from $136 billion in constant (FY2010) dollars in 1940 to $608 billion in 2010.[4]

Congress exercises control over federal grants through the authorization process which generally establishes key components of the grant program, including the funding allocation methodology, program eligibility, and congressional objectives. The allocation of federal grant funds is typically based on either statutory formula, agency discretion, or a combination of the two. In some cases, Congress establishes a formula for distributing funds that provides minimum allocations to primary grant recipients. In other cases, the formula establishes the percentage of funds that go to each grant recipient. The authorizing statute establishes the terms and conditions for the particular grant program. Federal agencies implement the statutory requirements in their regulations and incorporate them in grant agreements. A grant program may authorize a range of eligible activities. Congress may limit the grant project eligibility by narrowing the range of activities to address specific categories of projects. These types of grants are known as categorical grants. Congress may also choose to provide greater flexibility in the range of eligible grant activities by authorizing a block grant. Block grants allow recipients, predominately states, to fund a broad range of activities within more general policy areas such as community development or law enforcement.

The authorizing legislation also determines the level of federal agency discretion in administering the grant program. Federal agency discretion plays a critical role in the degree of transparency in federal grant program administration.

Mechanisms for Achieving Transparency: Pre-Award Process

For the purposes of this testimony, transparency is defined as the availability of information captured or created during the administration of the grant program. For some grant administration activities, transparency is analyzed from the perspective of the grant applicant and is measured by the clarity and conciseness of the information. In other cases, transparency is analyzed from the congressional perspective and is measured by the ability of Congress to conduct oversight. For grant applicants, lack of transparency may result in wasted resources pursing a federal grant. For agencies, lack of transparency may result in an inability to assess internal controls. For

Congress, lack of transparency may result in the inability to measure the efficiency, effectiveness, and economy of federal grant programs.

Establishing and Defining Criteria for Evaluation: What Information is Available

Federal agencies have discretion in determining the evaluation criteria for discretionary grants. Discretionary grants are awarded through a competitive process. The evaluation criteria used to prioritize the grant applications varies across programs and agencies. While agencies are required to provide evaluation criteria in the Notice of Funds Availability (NOFA) published in the Federal Register, the description generally does not include a concise list of the factors, and the weighted values of the factors, in the evaluation criteria.

Announcement of Funding Availability

The grantor agency publishes a NOFA in the Federal Register for each grant program. The NOFA provides application deadlines, eligibility information and grant evaluation criteria. Transparency in the award process begins with the clarity and conciseness of the information in the NOFA. Lack of clarity in the evaluation criteria may cause some applicants to provide insufficient information in the grant application, which would reduce the likelihood of the application receiving a grant award. Yet some agencies do not provide the evaluation information in a clear and concise manner.[5]

Establishing and Defining Formulas: Determining How Much is Awarded

Congress establishes the allocation methodology in the authorizing legislation for entitlement and formula grants. While the allocation methodology may provide the factors to be included in the formula, the agencies have discretion in determining what sources of information are used to assign a value to the factor. There is currently no single source providing information on the factors, weight of the factors in the overall formula, and acceptable sources of information for each factor. This was not always the case.

Impact of the Discontinuation of the Formula Report to the Congress

The Administrator of GSA is responsible for maintaining and providing wide access to a computerized information system on domestic assistance programs, and preparing, publishing, and distributing the most current information available through the catalog of federal domestic assistance programs each year.[6] GSA currently maintains the federal assistance information database that is publically accessible through www.cfda.gov. At one time, the GSA Administrator was also required to transmit to specified congressional committees the following information:

- Specification of each formula governing eligibility for assistance or the distribution of assistance under each program;
- Description of all data and statistical estimates used to carry out each formula; and
- Identification of the sources of such data and estimates.

In response to this mandate, GSA developed a report, *Formula Report to the Congress*, which it provided to Congress on an annual basis. GSA defined formula as, "any prescribed method employing objective data or statistical estimates for making individual determinations among recipients of federal funds either in terms of eligibility or actual funding allocations that can be written in the form of either a closed mathematical statement, or an iterative procedure or algorithm which can be written as a computer program."[7]

The report was discontinued as a result of the Federal Reports Elimination and Sunset Act of 1995.[8] The *1999 Formula Reports to the Congress* was the final report provided to Congress.

The *Formula Report to the Congress* was a potentially useful grants oversight tool because it could be used to conduct policy analysis such as evaluating the use of population factors in federal grant programs.[9] There is no other comparable federal report that provides this level of detail on federal grant formulas.

Establishing and Defining Eligible Activities: What Gets Funded

The degree to which federal agency discretion influences eligible activities varies depending on the type of grant program. As mentioned earlier, when Congress authorizes a federal grant program, the eligible activities may be broad or specific depending on the statutory language in the grant authorization. When grant funds are distributed through a competitive process, the administering federal agency officials exercise discretion in the selection of grant projects to be awarded funding within the range of eligible activities set forth by Congress.

Reviewing Applications: Determining Who and What Gets Funded

Grantor agencies have discretion in determining what information obtained during the screening and peer review process is disclosed. Grant applications are screened for eligibility, completeness, and timely submission. Grant applications that meet all of these requirements are then given further consideration. For some agencies, this may include a peer review. Some federal agencies utilize a panel of experts to review and score grant applications based on established criteria published in the NOFA. Some agencies contract out the review panel process, while others utilize internal program specialists. Potential criticism of review panels include a possible conflict of interest when a member of the panel has a professional or financial interest in selecting one grant project over another, ineffective implementation of the panel recommendations when projects are selected by agency officials regardless of the panel scores, and lack of uniformity in the procedures used to establish and implement review panels.

The disclosure of information obtained during the screening and review process varies from agency to agency. For example, some agencies provide the number of applicants and number of applications awarded on the agency website. Other agencies do not. Most agencies do not publish the review panel scores used to make final award decisions. Additionally, agency officials have discretion to make award decisions that do not exactly align with the review panel scores. While agency officials often must provide written justification when deviating from the review panel scores when making award decisions, the justification is an internal control and is seldom made publically available.

Oversight of federal agency grants administration activities is limited by the lack of transparency in the award process. Without knowledge of the individual application scores, it is impossible to determine the appropriateness of award decisions. When specific programs are investigated by the Government Accountability Office (GAO) or the agency's Office of Inspector General, the scores can be ascertained. However, on occasion, these investigations have found that grant award decisions were not predicated on the review panel scores. The following IG findings provide examples of discretion in the peer review process.

Department of Justice, Juvenile Justice Grants

In September 2009, the Inspector General of DOJ reported on an investigation into the awarding of juvenile justice grants.[10] There was media and congressional interest in the awarding of these grants prior to the IG involvement. In January 2008, a trade journal, *Youth Today*, reported that grants awarded under the National Juvenile Justice Program were not awarded competitively and that the administrator of the Office of Juvenile Justice and Delinquency Prevention (OJJDP), J. Robert Flores, had hand-picked the grant recipients.[11] On June 19, 2008, the House Committee on Oversight and Government Reform held a hearing titled, *Examining Grantmaking Practices at the Department of Justice.*[12] In his opening statement, then Chairman Henry A.Waxman indicated that while the Committee acknowledges that Administrator Flores has discretion in awarding federal grants, "he has an obligation to make these decisions based on merit, facts, and fairness."[13] The DOJ IG findings concurred with the discretion held by the administrator to select the grant award recipients, but stated that by not taking the review board recommendations into consideration, the administrator wasted agency resources.[14] Further, the IG found that, "the absence of earmarks in FY2007, coupled with a lack of applicable grant selection rules, gave the Office of Justice Programs considerable latitude in determining the organizations that should receive awards."[15] The IG recommended that DOJ implement peer review protocols that include consensus calls to discuss and mediate disparate peer review results and require at least three peer reviewers on each panel.[16]

Department of Education

In September 2006, the ED IG presented a report of the investigation of the composition of expert review panels utilized in awarding the Reading First grant to determine whether the panels were selected in accordance with the No Child Left Behind Act (NCLB), whether the panel members were screened for conflict of interest, whether the panel appropriately documented its decisions, and whether the panel reviewed the applications in accordance with established criteria. The IG concluded that ED did not select the review panel in compliance with the requirements in NCLB, the screening process for panel members to evaluate the risk of conflict of interest was not effective, that ED awarded grants without documentation, that the panel approved the selection criteria, and that ED did not follow its own guidance for a peer review process.[17] The IG recommended that the agency develop internal management policies and procedures that address when legal advice will be sought from the Office of General Counsel (OGC). Further, the IG recommended that the agency rely on an internal advisory committee to determine whether the implementation of the Reading First program harmed the federal interest and assess a course of action to resolve the issues identified. The IG recommended that the internal advisory committee be comprised of representatives from other ED programs, the OGC, and the Department's Risk Management Team.

Disclosing Proprietary or Confidential Information: What Will Be Disclosed

Disclosure is a key element of transparency. Disclosing information obtained by the agency in the screening and evaluation phase of grants administration, is tempered by the limitations some agencies impose on the disclosure of propriety information. This is particularly true for applications that were unsuccessful in seeking federal funding. Some agencies have established policies and procedures that will allow disclosure of information contained in a proposal that was not selected for funding only with the consent of the grant application.[18] Even when funds have been awarded, there are safeguards to protect proprietary or privileged information, including patentable ideas, trade secrets, or privileged or confidential information where the disclosure of which may harm the grant recipient.[19] Additionally, some grant programs may fund projects that require a degree of confidentiality. For example, the preparedness grants administered by the Department of Homeland Security fund homeland security prevention and protection activities. Disclosure of the nature of terrorist preparedness activities may pose a threat to national security since it would also provide insight into what types of activities are currently not being undertaken. Disclosure of grant application information must be balanced with measures to ensure protection of proprietary or privileged information while still achieving the goals of transparency.

CONCLUDING OBSERVATIONS

Federal agencies exercise discretion in a variety of ways when selecting recipients of federal grants. While there is general guidance in the OMB Circulars such as Circular A-110 which contain language that certain federal grants should be awarded on a competitive basis, this guidance is superseded by the statutory language in the authorizing legislation. Further, the interpretation of what constitutes "competitive" is often left to the federal administering agencies, as highlighted in the IG report concerning Administrator Flores and the DOJ Juvenile Justice grants. At times, the statutory language concerning allocation of federal grants creates tension by requiring the timely distribution of grant funds while also requiring selection of projects in a competitive manner.

Some agencies resolve this tension by using language in the regulations or the grant program guidance that gives priority consideration to projects that are able to be undertaken within a short period of time. This regulatory or guidance language may result in projects that may be more competitive to be passed over in favor of projects that are less competitive but more developed at the time applications are accepted. As highlighted by the examples above, the award process for federal grants lacks uniformity within and across federal agencies. This is due, in part, to the complexity and variation of the statutory language in grant authorizations. The variation may also be due to the uniqueness of the objectives of the grant programs.

An examination of the activities agencies undertake in the administration of federal grants, and the level of discretion exercised during those activities, can inform the oversight decisions. Further examination may be necessary to determine whether increased agency discretion warrants increased transparency.

I thank you for the opportunity to testify and would be happy to answer any questions the committee may have.

End Notes

[1] U.S. Congress, House Committee on Post Office and Civil Service, Subcommittee on Census and Population, *Federal Formula Grants-In-Aid Programs That Use Population As A Factor In Allocating Funds*, committee print, 94th Congress, 1st Sess., 94-6 (Washington: GPO, 1975), p. 4.

[2] U.S. Office of Management and Budget, *Managing Federal Assistance in the 1980s*, Mar. 1980, p. 18.

[3] Catalog of Federal Domestic Assistance, April 11, 2011, at www.cfda.gov.

[4] U.S. Office of Management and Budget, *Total Outlays for Grants to State and Local Governments by Function, Agency, and Program: 1940 – 2010*, (Washington: GPO, 2012), at http://www.whitehouse.gov/omb/budget/Historicals.

[5] U.S. Government Accountability Office, *Runaway and Homeless Youth Grants: Improvements Needed in the Grant Award Process*, GAO-10-335, May 2010, at http://www.gao.gov/new.items/d10335.pdf.

[6] P.L. 98-169.

[7] U.S. General Services Administration, *1999 Formula Report to the Congress*. This report is no longer in print but is available from CRS upon request.

[8] P.L. 104-66. Federal reports that were not specifically identified as exempted from the provisions of the act were discontinued.

[9] CRS Report RL30358, *Population Factors Used in Federal Assistance Programs*, by James R. Riehl.

[10] U.S. Department of Justice, Office of Inspector General, *Procedures Used by the Office of Juvenile Justice and Delinquency Prevention to Award Discretionary Grants in Fiscal Year 2007*, Audit Report 09-24, April 2009.

[11] Patrick Boyle, "For Juvenile Justice, A Panel of One," *Youth Today: The Newspaper on Youth Work*, December/January 2008, p.6.

[12] U.S. Congress, House Committee on Oversight and Government Reform, *Examining Grantmaking Practices at the Department of Justice*, 110th Cong., 2nd session, June 19, 2008 (Washington: GPO, 2008).

[13] Ibid, p. 3.

[14] U.S. Department of Justice, Office of Inspector General, *Procedures Used by the Office of Juvenile Justice and Delinquency Prevention to Award Discretionary Grants in Fiscal Year 2007*, Audit Report 09-24, April 2009, p. v. According to the IG report, DOJ paid a contractor more than $500,000 to oversee and conduct peer reviews of grant proposals.

[15] Ibid, p. iv.

[16] Ibid, p. 42.

[17] U.S. Department of Education, Office of Inspector General, *Final Inspection Report*, ED-OIG/I13-F0017, Sept. 2006.

[18] The National Science Foundation, Proposal and Award Policies and Procedures Guide, October 2010, p. I-4.

[19] Ibid.

In: Federal Grant Management
Editor: Vanessa N. Rowley

ISBN: 978-1-62100-185-0

Chapter 4

TESTIMONY OF DANNY I. WERFEL, CONTROLLER, OFFICE OF FEDERAL FINANCIAL MANAGEMENT BEFORE THE SUBCOMMITTEE ON TECHNOLOGY, INFORMATION POLICY, INTERGOVERNMENTAL RELATIONS AND PROCUREMENT REFORM COMMITTEE, HEARING ON "OVERSIGHT AND GOVERNMENT REFORM"*

Thank you Chairman Lankford, Ranking Member Connolly, and members of the Subcommittee, for the invitation to discuss with you today the Federal grant management process and how the Federal Government can improve oversight and accountability in federal grant programs.

The Federal Government has a fundamental responsibility to be an effective steward of taxpayers' money. This requires Federal agencies to implement rigorous financial management policies and controls to ensure that Federal funds are appropriately accounted for and wisely spent in accordance with laws and regulation. The Office of Management and Budget (OMB),

* This is an edited, reformatted and augmented version of testimony given by Danny I. Werfel, Controller, Office of Federal Financial Management before the Subcommittee on Technology, Information Policy, Intergovernmental Relations and Procurement Reform Committee, Hearing on "Oversight and Government Reform" on June 23, 2011.

working with Federal grant-making agencies and non-Federal stakeholders, has established policies and guidelines through OMB's grant management circulars and government–wide administrative common rules, codified by each grant-making agency. These policies and guidelines provide Federal agencies a solid framework to ensure that relevant program requirements are being met; that strong internal controls for reducing waste, fraud, and error are in place; and that grantees are meeting their responsibility for performance and accountability for the grant awards.

A substantial amount of Federal funding is obligated each year through the awarding of grants. The Federal Government annually awards grants totaling more than $500 billion, one-sixth of the total Federal budget. In 2010, total grant awards were $572 billion, including grants funded under the American Recovery and Reinvestment Act of 2009 (Recovery Act) as compared to $309 billion in awards granted in 2000. Thus within 10 years, grant awards have grown by 85%. The Catalog of Federal Domestic Assistance lists more 2,000 Federal assistance programs, including both formula and competitive grant programs administered by more than 30 Federal agencies. State and local governments and Indian tribes received 83% of the grant awards in 2010, while other grantees (colleges, universities, non-profit organizations, for-profit organizations) received 17% of the grant awards.

Over the last decade and commensurate with the substantial increase in the volume of grant awards, there has also been an increase in the efforts improve management of grants by making easier for applicants to find and apply for grant opportunities. The Federal Financial Assistance Management Improvement Act of 1999 required the development of an electronic solution to support the grants management process. The Grants.gov solution was developed in response to this law, providing a central portal for applicants to find and apply for grant opportunities. Although the deployment of this solution represents a major milestone in the streamlining and modernization of the grant application process, Grants.gov has historically experienced system outages and slow processing times, the most pronounced occurring in the months leading up to the passage of the Recovery Act. Due to these technical difficulties, and the anticipated spike in application volume expected when the Recovery Act awards would be made available, OMB directed Federal agencies to begin accepting applications through alternative electronic means to reduce the strain on Grants.gov. This decision proved effective as the Federal grant application process worked smoothly even with the increased activity spurred by the Recovery Act. At that time, additional funding was provided to stabilize the system, which resulted in the purchase of additional servers. Today, all Federal agencies are back to using Grants.gov and the solution has a quicker response time and can process more simultaneous applications than in previous years. We are currently exploring ways to further improve the platform to further simplify the grant application process, especially for applicants with multiple grants at different agencies.

To ensure proper grant management and the accountability of Federal grant dollars, OMB has issued grant management circulars and other policies and guidelines for Federal agencies to apply throughout the life cycle of a grant, including pre-award requirements, post-award requirements, guidelines for determining allowable and unallowable costs by grantees, and audit requirements for grantees. The circulars, policies, and guidelines provide a solid foundation for mitigating waste, fraud, and abuse, such as unallowable or unallocable costs charged to Federal programs. Furthermore, in order to improve transparency regarding government-wide grant policy for the grantees, OMB established a new title in the Code of Federal Regulations – Title 2, Grants and Agreements, that include both OMB guidance and agency implementation regulations. Title 2 ensures greater uniformity and standardization in grant processes, reducing the potential for waste, fraud and abuse.

In particular, the Single Audit is the primary tool that Federal agencies use for overseeing their grant programs. The Single Audit Act of 1984 (further amended in 1996, 31 U.S.C. 7501) provides for a cost-effective audit in lieu of multiple audits and for combining the annual financial statement audit with the review and testing of the grantee's internal controls and compliance with requirements of major programs. Under OMB's implementing guidance of OMB Circular A-133, "Audits of States, Local Governments, and Non-Profit Organizations," grantees with $500,000 expenditures or more in Federal awards in a given year must obtain an annual audit of their activities. Under these requirements, more than 40,000 grantees (covering over 95% of all Federal grant expenditures) are audited annually. The audit results, including an opinion on the reviewed Federal programs, are available on a public website maintained by the Federal Audit Clearinghouse.[1]

[1] The Federal Audit Clearinghouse (FAC), operated by the Bureau of Census, serves as the central collection point, repository, and distribution center for single audit reports. See http://harvester.census.gov/fac/. Single audit results are entered into this national database so that audit findings can be tracked by program, State, or grantee. The FAC database is on-line, fully automated, assessable by the public for information from single audit reports and findings nationwide, and provides a cost-effective way for grantees to submit reports to the Federal government as required by law.

When Single Audits are conducted effectively and Federal agencies require prompt corrective action, the audit results are instrumental in identifying and correcting any non-compliance with laws and regulations (including improper payments), lack of internal controls, adequacy of drawdown and reimbursement requests, compliance with financial and program reporting, adequacy of subgrantee oversight, and other financial management deficiencies. A good example is in the Medicaid program, where more than a billion dollars in disallowed costs have been identified for recovery over the past several years as a result of Single Audit activities.

While progress has been made in grants management, there remain further opportunities to standardize and streamline the management process and enhance efforts to mitigate waste, fraud, and abuse. In particular, we will build on a foundation of progress being achieved under the Administration's Accountable Government Initiative (AGI) as well as the lessons learned from the successful execution of Recovery Act awards.

Through the AGI, the Federal Government is eliminating inefficient and duplicative programs, cutting contracting costs, eliminating improper payments, improving investments in information technology, and disposing of unneeded Federal real estate. These efforts have led to billions of dollars in savings and efficiencies to date, and in each area, Federal agencies are executing on plans to achieve additional savings in the short term. Further, as noted by a broad array of government leaders, Congressional stakeholders, and external observers, Recovery Act funds were awarded on a timely basis, with low levels of fraud and error, and with unprecedented transparency.

Building on these various successes, the President recently signed the Executive Order, "Delivering an Efficient, Effective, and Accountable Government." Among other provisions, the Order announced the establishment of a new accountability board, the Government Accountability and Transparency Board (GATB), to help federal agencies improve their performance and reduce waste, fraud and abuse across government. Bringing the tools and very successful efforts of the Recovery Accountability and Transparency Board (RATB) to the rest of government spending, the GATB will:

- Provide oversight and strategic direction to enhance the transparency of Federal spending, including the collection, display, and reliability of government spending data; and

- Advance efforts to detect and remediate fraud and waste in Federal programs, including the deployment of fraud detection technologies that proved successful during the implementation of the Recovery Act.

The GATB will jointly engage both agencies and Inspectors General on these efforts toward the common goal of enhanced transparency and accountability. In addition, the creation of the GATB provides an opportunity to help drive a new and more robust governance structure for the grants community. Specifically, there are currently numerous boards, councils, and committees with current responsibilities for providing strategic direction to the grants community. With the GATB in place, there is an opportunity to coordinate these activities and pursue a more singular vision toward effective accountability of Federal grant awards. In the near term, we hope to achieve a new and unified grants governance framework, aligned and coordinated with the GATB.

Fortunately, and as noted above, ongoing activities under the AGI and the Recovery Act provide a strong foundation for reform and improvement in the area of grants management. I would like to spend the remainder of my testimony highlighting three of these areas.

Improper Payments Prevention and Recapture

The Federal Government's payment error rate declined in FY 2010, helping Federal agencies avoid roughly $4 billion in improper payments. Eliminating improper payments has been a major focus of this Administration. In November, 2009, the President issued an Executive Order that initiated a comprehensive approach to improving results in this area, including improved transparency through a new improper payment website, Payment Accuracy.gov, and the appointment of senior accountable officials responsible for coordinating improper payment efforts at agencies with high incidences of payment errors. Following the Executive Order, the President issued a directive requiring Federal agencies to increase recoveries of erroneous Federal payments to contractors. As a result of this directive, Federal agencies recovered $687 million in improper payments to contractors, triple the amount of payment recoveries from the prior year. Last summer, the President signed bipartisan legislation, the Improper Payment Elimination and Recovery Act (IPERA), which strengthens accountability with respect to all aspects of improper payments and provides new authorities to assist Federal agencies in recovering erroneous payments to grantees. Most recently, in April, OMB released IPERA's implementing guidance, and agencies are now complying with the new law and implementing guidance, including the expansion of payment recapture audits to grantees.

FRAUD TECHNOLOGY PILOTS

To further mitigate waste, fraud, and abuse, OMB has worked with the RATB and Federal agencies to utilize cutting edge fraud detection capabilities to enhance accountability and eliminate fraud in Federal award spending. OMB, the RATB, and the Centers for Medicare and Medicaid Services (CMS) have piloted a broader application of the RATB's fraud detection tool to awards funded with non-Recovery Act funds. This pilot project was extremely successful, as the Recovery Board's tool helped uncover instances of fraud in CMS programs. As a result, CMS recently announced plans to expand its use of forensic tools to more aggressively go after fraud. In addition, OMB and the Department of the Treasury, in close consultation with the RATB, are currently in the process of expanding VerifyPayment.gov to include a "Do Not Pay" portal, which will provide agencies with the capability to do pre-award validation checks against relevant existing databases across the Federal Government to verify a recipient's eligibility before award and payment. These two efforts will not only help to prevent waste, fraud, and abuse up front prior to awarding a grant but also provide the capability to detect fraud after the grant has been awarded.

SUB-AWARD REPORTING

Bolstered by the successful transparency initiatives under the Recovery Act, OMB initiated requirements for the reporting of sub-award information on all Federal spending. Through the USAspending.gov platform, the public has increased visibility into Federal spending, beyond the prime recipient level. As of June 2011, for awards made beginning in 2000, USAspending.gov displays over $25.4 trillion in prime awards, based on over 48,000 individual prime awards, and over $1.4 trillion in sub-awards.

The Administration remains committed to continuing efforts to improve the grant management process and identification and mitigation of waste, fraud, and abuse. We are also in the early stages of developing improvements to Single Audits that will eliminate unnecessary burden while improving the rigor of the audit itself. Further, we are developing a new set of performance metrics in the area of Single Audit that will help ensure that Federal programs and recipients are held accountable for resolving audit findings quickly and effectively.

We look forward to working closely with this Committee toward the effective implementation of current and future transparency and accountability efforts to ensure that Federal grant programs are accountable for taxpayer dollars.

Thank you again for the opportunity to testify today. I look forward to answering your questions.

In: Federal Grant Management
Editor: Vanessa N. Rowley
ISBN: 978-1-62100-185-0

Chapter 5

STATEMENT OF THOMAS A. COBURN, M.D., U.S. SENATOR, OKLAHOMA BEFORE THE HOUSE SUBCOMMITTEE ON TECHNOLOGY, INFORMATION POLICY, INTERGOVERNMENTAL RELATIONS AND PROCUREMENT REFORM, HEARING ON "IMPROVING OVERSIGHT AND ACCOUNTABILITY IN FEDERAL GRANT PROGRAMS"*

Thank you Chairman Lankford, Ranking Member Connolly and distinguished members of the Committee for inviting me to testify about oversight of our federal grant programs, especially as relates to the grant-making process at the National Science Foundation (NSF).

Every year, hundreds of billions of taxpayer dollars are lost to waste, fraud, abuse and mismanagement. As an elected official, I take seriously my duty to safeguard taxpayers' investments in federal programs by ensuring their money is used effectively, efficiently and for sound purposes. This is for an

* This is an edited, reformatted and augmented version of a Thomas A. Coburn, M.D., U.S. Senator, Oklahoma before the House Subcommittee on Technology, Information Policy, Intergovernmental Relations and Procurement Reform, Hearing on "Improving Oversight and Accountability in Federal Grant Programs" publication, dated on Thursday, June 23, 2011.

important reason: when the government recklessly wastes taxpayer money, the public trust is undermined.

As part of my oversight efforts, I have released a series of reports examining various federal programs and agencies. The most recent in this series – National Science Foundation: Under the Microscope – identified more than $1.2 billion at NSF that has been lost to waste, fraud, duplication and mismanagement and an additional $1.7 billion in funds that have gone unused.

As a practicing physician and a two-time cancer survivor, I have a very personal appreciation for the benefits of scientific research. Investing in innovation and discovery can transform and improve our lives, advance our understanding of the world, and create meaningful new jobs.

While I am committed to targeted investments in transformative research, I believe the core mission of NSF is undermined when taxpayer dollars are wasted on frivolous and low-priority efforts. I believe taxpayers share my skepticism regarding the priority of recent NSF studies such as: How long can shrimp run on a treadmill; How to ride a bike; When did dogs became man's best friend; Why some college basketball teams dominate March Madness; If political views are genetically pre-determined; How to improve the quality of wine; Do boys like to play with trucks and girls like to play with dolls; How rumors get started; How much housework does a husband create for a wife; and When is the best time to buy a ticket to a sold out sporting event.

While many of the examples highlighted in my recent report are entertaining, they are also symptoms of a broken grant-making process in need of reform:

POOR GRANT ADMINISTRATION LEAVES $1.7 BILLION IN LIMBO

According to NSF's 2010 financial statements, the agency currently has $1.733 billion in "undisbursed balances in expired grant accounts."[1] The over $1.7 billion of NSF funds that remain in limbo means, in practical terms, less money for research.

Agency policy is to close out grant awards on the award expiration date. One quarter later, any un-liquidated funds are to be de-obligated. [2] NSF then identifies funding to be returned to the Treasury from any cancelled appropriations. In 2010, NSF returned $33.68 million to the United States Treasury while sitting on $1.7 billion in undisbursed, expired funding. The

NSF's Work Faces Extensive Duplication Challenges, Both within the Agency and Across the Federal Government

NSF is one of at least 15 federal departments, 72 sub-agencies, and 12 independent agencies engaged in federal research and development.[20] An NSF-led analysis of the federal research budget explains that the federal government has, "17 science agencies [that] have 17 different data silos, with different identifiers, different reporting structures, and different sets of metrics."[21]

NSF also duplicates the work of the U.S. Department of Education and other government departments and agencies in the area of Science, Technology, Engineering, and Mathematics (STEM) education. In Fiscal Year 2010, there were 28 STEM education programs at NSF totaling $1.2 billion (Appendix 1).[22] According to a May 2007 report of the Academic Competitiveness Council (ACC), there are 105 federal programs supporting STEM education, with aggregate funding of $3.2 billion in FY 2006.[23]

In conclusion, at a time when the U.S. is being both challenged as the world's scientific and technological leader and threatened by a nearly insurmountable $14 trillion debt, we must learn to do more with less, and to do so efficiently and effectively.

I have recently communicated with NSF Director Dr. Subra Suresh and I know he shares a commitment to better prioritizing our nation's limited financial resources to advance science and reduce wasteful spending. I plan to support his efforts in this regard, and encourage members of this Subcommittee to do the same.

Thank you again for inviting me to take part in this important conversation. I look forward to any questions you may have for me.

End Notes

[1] National Science Foundation 2011 Financial Statements, "Chapter 3: Appendices, http://www.nsf.gov/pubs/2011/nsf11003/pdf/chapter3appendices.pdf (March 16,2011).

[2] National Science Foundation 2011 Financial Statements, "Chapter 3: Appendices, http://www.nsf.gov/pubs/2011/nsf11003/pdf/chapter3appendices.pdf (March 16,2011).

[3] National Science Foundation 2011 Financial Statements, "Chapter 3: Appendices, page III-24, http://www.nsf.gov/pubs/2011/nsf11003/pdf/chapter3appendices.pdf (March 16,2011).

[4] Government Accountability Office, "GRANTS MANAGEMENT; Attention Needed to Address Undisbursed Balances in Expired Grant Accounts," August 2008, Page 2; http://www.gao.gov/new.items/d08432.pdf

[5] Government Accountability Office, "GRANTS MANAGEMENT; Attention Needed to Address Undisbursed Balances in Expired Grant Accounts," August 2008, Page 5; http://www.gao.gov/new.items/d08432.pdf

[6] Statement Of Allison C. Lerner, Inspector General, National Science Foundation, Before The House Commerce, Justice, Science Appropriations Subcommittee, February 2011,http://www.nsf.gov/oig/testimonyfeb2011.pdf (March 11, 2011).

[7] Statement Of Allison C. Lerner, Inspector General, National Science Foundation, Before The House Commerce, Justice, Science Appropriations Subcommittee, February 2011,http://www.nsf.gov/oig/testimonyfeb2011.pdf (March 11, 2011).

[8] Statement Of Allison C. Lerner, Inspector General, National Science Foundation, Before The House Commerce, Justice, Science Appropriations Subcommittee, February 2011, http://www.nsf.gov/oig/testimonyfeb2011.pdf (March 11, 2011).

[9] Statement Of Allison C. Lerner, Inspector General, National Science Foundation, Before The House Commerce, Justice, Science Appropriations Subcommittee, February 2011, http://www.nsf.gov/oig/testimonyfeb2011.pdf (March 11, 2011).

[10] Statement Of Allison C. Lerner, Inspector General, National Science Foundation, Before The House Commerce, Justice, Science Appropriations Subcommittee, February 2011, http://www.nsf.gov/oig/testimonyfeb2011.pdf (March 11, 2011).

[11] NSF/OIG Semiannual Report to Congress, "FY 2011 Top Management Challenges & Back Matter," September 2010, http://www.nsf.gov/pubs/2011/oig11001/oig110017.pdf (January 26, 2011).

[12] NSF/OIG Semiannual Report to Congress, "FY 2011 Top Management Challenges & Back Matter," September 2010, http://www.nsf.gov/pubs/2011/oig11001/oig110017.pdf (January 26, 2011).

[13] Office of Inspector General, "Audit of Project Reporting for NSF Awards ," National Science Foundation December 13, 2004, OIG 05-2-006, http://www.nsf.gov/oig/newsletter/032005.htm#one (January 26, 2011).

[14] Office of Inspector General, "Audit of Project Reporting for NSF Awards ," National Science Foundation December 13, 2004, OIG 05-2-006, http://www.nsf.gov/oig/05-2-006Final.pdf (January 26, 2011).

[15] Office of Inspector General, "Audit of Project Reporting for NSF Awards ," National Science Foundation December 13, 2004, OIG 05-2-006, http://www.nsf.gov/oig/05-2-006Final.pdf (January 26, 2011).

[16] Office of Inspector General, "Audit of Project Reporting for NSF Awards ," National Science Foundation December 13, 2004, OIG 05-2-006, http://www.nsf.gov/oig/newsletter/032005.htm#one (January 26, 2011).

[17] Office of Inspector General, "Audit of Project Reporting for NSF Awards ," National Science Foundation December 13, 2004, OIG 05-2-006, http://www.nsf.gov/oig/newsletter/032005.htm#one (January 26, 2011).

[18] Email Correspondence between the National Science Foundation Congressional Affairs Office and the staff of Senator Tom Coburn, March 16, 2011.

[19] NSF/OIG Semiannual Report to Congress, "FY 2011 Top Management Challenges & Back Matter," September 2010, http://www.nsf.gov/pubs/2011/oig11001/index.jsp (January 26, 2011).

[20] National Science Foundation, "Survey of Federal Funds for Research and Development," Last updated June 2009, http://www.nsf.gov/statistics (April 4, 2011).

[21] Julia Lane and Stefano Bertuzzi, "The STAR METRICS Project: Current and Future Uses for S&E Workforce Data," The National Science Foundation and the National Institutes of Health, June 2010, http://www.nsf.gov/sbe/sosp/workforce

[22] To gather the STEM program funding numbers for Fiscal Year 2010, staff used the Academic Competitiveness Council (ACC) report on STEM programs from 2007 as a guide. To find the current numbers, staff used each of the agencies FY 2010 budget documents and recorded the funding levels for each program specified by the ACC study. While updating the numbers from the 2007 report, staff searched for any new agency programs pertaining to STEM, or a specific science, technology, mathematics, or engineering initiative. All programs and their funding levels are detailed in Appendix 1.

[23] U.S. Department of Education, "Report of the Academic Competitiveness Council, May 2007.

In: Federal Grant Management
Editor: Vanessa N. Rowley
ISBN: 978-1-62100-185-0

Chapter 6

GRANTS.GOV: ADDITIONAL ACTION NEEDED TO ADDRESS PERSISTENT GOVERNANCE AND FUNDING CHALLENGES*

United States Government Accountability Office

WHY GAO DID THIS STUDY

In response to the Federal Financial Assistance Management Improvement Act of 1999, the Office of Management and Budget (OMB), among other things, deployed Grants.gov as the central grant identification and application portal for federal grant programs in 2003 and named the Department of Health and Human Services (HHS) its managing partner. As a result of funding and governance challenges— such as untimely contributions, a lack of performance metrics, unclear lines of authority, and confusion over roles and responsibilities among Grants.gov's governance bodies— that have adversely affected operations, GAO is required to examine (1) key factors HHS should consider when proposing a funding model for Grants.gov, and (2) how the Grants.gov governance bodies could address Grants.gov's previously identified governance challenges. To do this, GAO analyzed agency

* This is an edited, reformatted and augmented version of the United States Government Accountability Office publication, Report to Congressional Committees GAO-11-478, dated May 2011.

documents and interviewed officials at HHS, OMB, the Grants Executive Board (GEB), three case study agencies that manage similar E-Gov initiatives and three Grants.gov partner agencies.

What GAO Recommends

GAO is making four recommendations to HHS aimed at improving Grants.gov's funding calculation, cost tracking, and annual and strategic plan; and knowledge-sharing with other E-Gov initiatives. HHS generally agreed with our findings and recommendations.

What GAO Found

In keeping with OMB's expectation to move toward a fee-for-service model, starting with the fiscal year 2010 budget, the Grants.gov contribution calculation changed to better reflect agencies' use of Grants.gov's services. However, GAO found that the calculation results in different contribution amounts for agencies with similar usage profiles because the calculation includes a measure of agency size that does not correlate well with an agency's use of Grants.gov. For example, usage data for the fiscal year 2011 contributions indicates that the Department of Housing and Urban Development (HUD, a large agency) posted 40 grant opportunities and received 4,817 applications through the Grants.gov Web site while the National Endowment for the Humanities (NEH, a small agency) posted 42 opportunities and received 4,577 applications. However, HUD's contribution is \$414,422 while NEH's is \$155,159. In addition, GAO found that the Grants.gov Program Management Office (PMO) does not track and report on certain key costs, limiting partner agencies' ability to understand the relationship between services received and amounts paid for that service. Grants.gov also does not charge partner agencies for all known costs, which can result in some agencies subsidizing other agencies' use of the system. Finally, Grants.gov continues to suffer from untimely agency contributions. While the other E-Gov initiatives GAO spoke with report similar challenges, some take mitigating steps that aid them in managing delays. They are: (1) depositing partner fees/contributions into multiyear appropriation accounts and

(2) receiving some form of funds from their managing partners until partner agency contributions become available.

Accountability and responsibility for Grants.gov performance among its governance bodies—the PMO, GEB and HHS's Office of the Chief Information Officer (OCIO)—remains unclear. Since GAO first reported on these issues in July 2009, some progress has been made clarifying roles and responsibilities, developing performance measures to track important aspects of system performance, and providing partner agencies with key performance and cost information. However, although the GEB and the OCIO continue to share responsibility for approving major changes to, and funding for, the Grants.gov system, there remains little evidence that the GEB-approved funding for Grants.gov is considered in HHS's review of Grants.gov as an IT investment as required by OMB guidance. In addition, Grants.gov's performance measures have not changed since GAO reported on them and still do not provide a clear picture of system performance. Finally, Grants.gov does not communicate some key performance and activity cost information with its partner agencies.

A new federal grants governance model under OMB review would merge various Grants.gov governance entities and serve as the federal grants advisory body responsible for establishing the direction for and coordinating all governmentwide grants initiatives, including Grants.gov. As a preliminary, concept document, it is understandable that it contains few implementation details; however, the proposal lacks even an overview of several critical elements, such as how grants initiatives would be managed as IT investments.

ABBREVIATIONS

CCB	Change Control Board
CFO	Chief Financial Officer
CIO	Chief Information Officer
CNCS	Corporation for National and Community Service
CPIC	Capital Planning and Investment Control
DAIP	Disaster Assistance Improvement Program
DHS	Department of Homeland Security
DOE	Department of Energy
DOI	Department of the Interior
DOL	Department of Labor
E-Gov	Electronic Government

FEMA	Federal Emergency Management Agency
FPDS	Federal Procurement Data System
FY	Fiscal Year
GEB	Grants Executive Board
GPC	Grants Policy Committee
GSA	General Services Administration
HHS	Department of Health and Human Services
HUD	Department of Housing and Urban Development
IAE	Integrated Acquisition Environment
IT	information technology
MOU	Memorandum of Understanding
NEH	National Endowment for the Humanities
OCIO	Office of the Chief Information Officer
OMB	Office of Management and Budget
PMO	Program Management Office

May 6, 2011

The Honorable Tom Harkin
Chairman

The Honorable Richard Shelby
Ranking Member
Subcommittee on Labor, Health and Human Services,
Education, and Related Agencies
Committee on Appropriations
United States Senate

The Honorable Denny Rehberg
Chairman

The Honorable Rosa Delauro
Ranking Member
Subcommittee on Labor, Health and Human Services,
Education, and Related Agencies
Committee on Appropriations
House of Representatives

Grants.gov[1] serves as the central grant identification and application portal for more than 1,000 federal grant programs that fund approximately $500 billion in grants from 26 grant-making agencies for activities such as training, research, planning, construction, and the provision of services in areas such as health care, education, transportation, and homeland security. However, as we have previously reported, the Department of Health and Human Services (HHS), Grants.gov's managing partner, has faced funding and governance challenges that have adversely affected Grants.gov operations.[2] For example, we said that Grants.gov's challenges had in some cases led to late or incomplete applications and lost opportunities for both grantees and the population that may have benefited from the grantee's programs and services. In March 2009, the Office of Management and Budget (OMB) also noted that the Grants.gov system had experienced periods of noticeably degraded performance and described the system as being at serious risk for failure. Concerned about the impending influx of Recovery Act-related grant applications, OMB instructed federal grant-making agencies with viable alternatives to identify temporary, alternate methods for accepting grant applications and in April 2009, instructed the agencies to cover the additional costs of urgent improvements to the system.[3] In a July 2009 report, we recommended that the Director of OMB work with HHS to develop Grants.gov system performance measures, guidance clarifying the governance structure, a structured means for applicant input, and uniform policies for processing grant applications. OMB and HHS generally agreed with our recommendations; while they have taken some steps to address them, they have not yet fully implemented the recommendations.

This report responds to a mandate to examine the Grants.gov system and make recommendations to improve system management, focusing on a business model that provides an adequate, reliable funding stream and the appointment of a unified administrative body that is delegated both control and resources. To accomplish this, we evaluated (1) key factors HHS should consider when proposing a funding model for Grants.gov, and (2) how the Grants.gov governance bodies could address Grants.gov's previously identified governance challenges. In order to address both objectives, we reviewed available reports and documentary evidence and conducted interviews with relevant officials from OMB, HHS, and the Grants Executive Board (GEB). To obtain further information for both objectives, we also selected three case study agencies—the Department of Labor (DOL), the Department of Homeland Security (DHS), and the General Services Administration (GSA)—all of which are managing partners of other E-

Government (E-Gov) initiatives identified by OMB as similar to Grants.gov. To draw on the experiences of these three managing partners, we reviewed available reports and documentary evidence and conducted interviews at DOL – managing partner of Benefits.gov (see app. II); DHS/Federal Emergency Management Agency (FEMA) – managing partner of Disaster Assistance Improvement Program (DAIP) (see app. III) and GSA – managing partner of Integrated Acquisition Environment (IAE) (see app. IV). Each of these initiatives have funding and governance models similar to those of Grants.gov. In addition, in order to obtain more information from the perspective of Grants.gov partner agencies, we interviewed relevant officials at the Departments of Homeland Security, Labor, and the Interior.

We conducted this performance audit from April 2010 to May 2011 in accordance with generally accepted government auditing standards. Those standards require that we plan and perform the audit to obtain sufficient, appropriate evidence to provide a reasonable basis for our findings and conclusions based on our audit objectives. We believe that the evidence obtained provides a reasonable basis for our findings and conclusions based on our audit objectives.

BACKGROUND

Over 1,000 federal grant programs are disbursed and managed by 26 federal agencies and other federal grant-making organizations. Because of concerns about the burden on grantees of the varying requirements imposed by these different grant programs, Congress enacted the Federal Financial Assistance Management Improvement Act of 1999, commonly referred to by the grants community and OMB as Public Law 106-107.[4] Among other things, the act also required OMB to direct, coordinate, and assist agencies in developing and implementing a common application and reporting system that included electronic processes with which a nonfederal entity can apply for multiple grant programs that serve similar purposes but are administered by different federal agencies.[5] In response to Public Law 106-107, among other things, OMB created Grants.gov (initially known as e-Grants), and included it among the initiatives designated in OMB's 2002 E-Government Strategy.[6] As these programs were initiated shortly after the E-Government Act of 2002 became law,[7] we refer to them in this report as legacy E-Gov initiatives. The Grants.gov Web site was deployed with both the "Find" and "Apply" tools on October 31, 2003, and was meant, in part, to improve the announcement and application stages (together known as the pre-award stage) of the grant-making process for grantees. OMB has directed that almost all federal discretionary grant opportunities should be posted to the Grants.gov Web site; applicants can search for grant opportunities by agency or across agencies using the "Find" mechanism. Many grant announcements include a link to application forms and instructions.

Grants.gov Governance

As with all legacy E-Gov initiatives, OMB established a management structure to oversee the initiative and to facilitate a collaborative working environment for Grants.gov. This management structure included a managing partner agency—HHS—to manage the system and to coordinate agency involvement in managing and developing procedures supporting the use of the system. The Grants.gov oversight and management structure also includes the GEB, and the Grants.gov Program Management Office (PMO).

Managing Partner Agency

As managing partner for Grants.gov, HHS is responsible for managing Grants.gov. HHS is also responsible for managing Grants.gov as an information technology (IT) investment through HHS's Office of the Chief Information Officer (OCIO). The OCIO is required to manage Grants.gov through HHS's capital programming and budget process. The HHS Office of Grants provides departmental input to Grants.gov and other governmentwide grant initiatives, and key leadership and oversight on Grants.gov management and implementation.

Grants Executive Board (GEB)

The GEB was established in 2002 at HHS's request to help coordinate agency involvement in managing Grants.gov and consists of grant-making officials from the 26 partner agencies. The GEB's role is to provide strategic leadership and resources to Grants.gov, including reviewing implementation and operational policies, the Grants.gov budget, and the level of financial contribution of each partner agency. The GEB charter states that it "will serve as an authoritative voice for the grant-making agencies, providing a governance body that can vote on proposals and deliverables as representatives of the grant-making agencies."

Grants.gov Program Management Office (PMO)

Day-to-day management of the Grants.gov initiative and its budget is the responsibility of the Grants.gov PMO, which is located within HHS and is currently staffed by 10 employees plus supporting contractor personnel. The PMO is also responsible for managing the process to update the standard grant application forms (SF 424 series) approved by OMB for governmentwide use.

In addition, the Grants Policy Committee (GPC), established by the Chief Financial Officers (CFO) Council, has overall responsibility for implementing Public Law 106-107. One of its goals is to "simplify federal financial assistance processes to make them more uniform across agencies and eliminate unnecessary burdens on applicants, grantees, and federal agencies." Specifically, the Grants Policy Committee is to, among other things, coordinate all federal grants policy recommendations submitted to OMB, recommend uniform forms and formats for grant applications and post-award reports, recommend standard and streamlined federal-to-grantee business processes, facilitate greater community input and outreach in streamlining federal financial assistance, and collaborate with the GEB on Grants.gov and other streamlining issues. The committee's pre-award working group is responsible for developing policy proposals for streamlining and simplifying the pre-award stage of the grants life cycle. Figure 1 illustrates the various entities involved in the grant pre-award stages at the federal level.

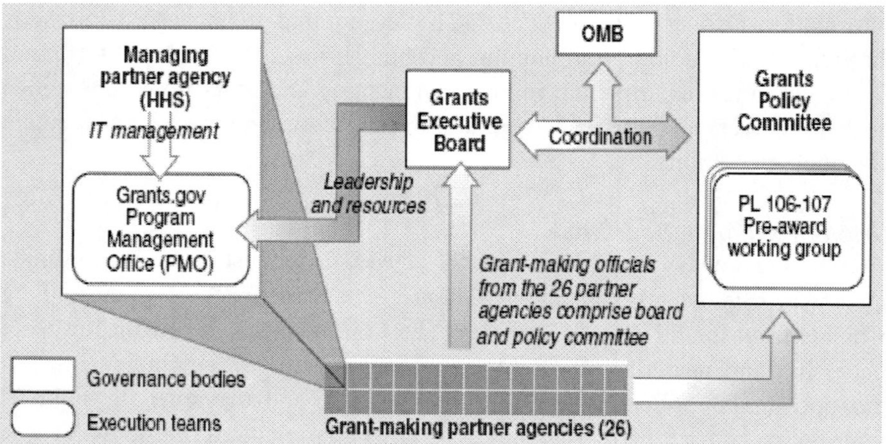

Source: GAO analysis of OMB data.

Figure 1. Entities Involved in the Federal Grants Pre-Award Stage of Grants Life Cycle.

Grants.gov Funding

The legacy E-Gov initiatives are funded using a variety of approaches, including partner agency contributions, fee-for-service, direct payments from the managing partner agency, or some combination of these. OMB defines contribution and fee-for-service models as follows:

- **Contribution model:** Commitments of funding and/or in-kind services provided by partner agencies to initiative managing partner agencies in support of developing, implementing, and/or migrating to E-Gov common solutions. Contribution amounts are determined annually through collaborative, interagency E-Gov initiative governance structures and subject to approval by OMB.
- **Fee-for-service model:** A transfer of funds by partner agencies to initiative service providers in exchange for services rendered by the initiative service providers. The amounts are typically based on a transaction/usage-based fee structure (e.g., for payroll processing, payroll service providers base their service fees on the number of employees at a customer agency). Initiative service providers use fees collected from partner agencies to cover ongoing operational costs, perform routine maintenance, and support their customer base.

In June 2004, OMB issued a memo detailing the Grants.gov funding model and partner agencies' Grants.gov contributions, as approved by the GEB.[8] Grants.gov is funded by payments from its 26 partner agencies. Memoranda of Understanding (MOUs) between the Grants.gov PMO and the partner agencies establish the amount and timing of the contributions to be made and the Grants.gov services to be provided. Annually, the GEB votes on both the Grants.gov budget and the calculation that will be used to determine each agency's payment.

Grants.gov Funding Model Raises Issues about How Costs Are Distributed among Users and the Lack of Effective Strategies to Manage Recurring Collection Delays

Grants.gov's Funding Model Attempts to Better Align Contributions with Agency Use

In keeping with OMB's expectation for legacy E-Gov initiatives to move toward a fee-for-service model, starting with the fiscal year 2010 budget, the Grants Executive Board (GEB) approved changes to the Grants.gov contribution calculation to better reflect agencies' use of Grants.gov's services partner agency charges are based on three factors (see fig. 2):

- charges based on agency size comprise 20 percent of the Grants.gov budget,
- charges based on the number of grant opportunities posted by an agency comprise 40 percent of the Grants.gov budget, and
- charges based on the number of grant applications submitted comprise 40 percent of the Grants.gov budget.

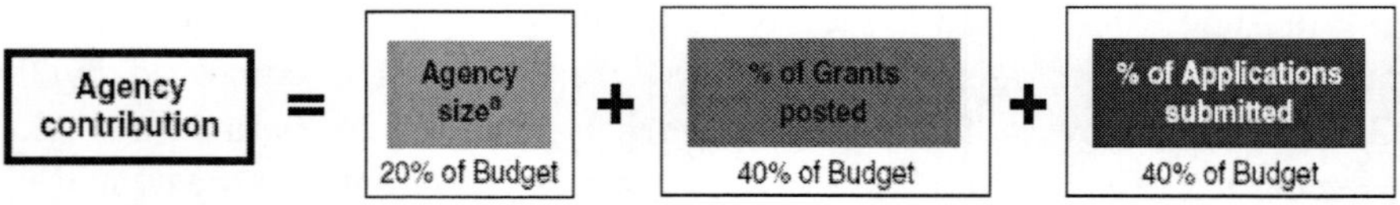

Source: GAO analysis of HHS data.

[a] Agency size, as measured in the contribution calculation, is based on an agency's total dollar value of discretionary grants.

Figure 2. Grants.gov Contribution Calculation.

To determine agency size for the purposes of Grants.gov, partner agencies are divided into five groups based on an agency's total dollar value of discretionary grants: extra small, small, medium, large, and extra large. The component of an agency's contribution based on agency size is the same for all agencies within a size category. For example, for fiscal year 2011 the agency size component of an agency's contribution is $50,000 for all small agencies and $200,000 for all large agencies.[9]

Two measures of Web site usage comprise the other two components of the contribution calculation: (1) an agency's share of total grant opportunities posted on Grants.gov, and (2) an agency's share of total grant applications submitted through Grants.gov. According to fiscal year 2007 data—on which the GEB based its fiscal year 2011 calculations— agencies posted from 3 to 1,167 grant opportunities on Grants.gov. Grant applications submitted through Grants.gov ranged from 13 to 107,961.[10]

The Grants.gov Contribution Calculation Results in Different Contribution Amounts for Agencies with Similar System Use

The Grants.gov contribution calculation results in different contribution amounts for agencies with similar usage profiles. For example, under the fiscal year 2011 contribution calculation, the Department of Housing and Urban Development (categorized as a large agency for the purposes of Grants.gov) posted 40 grant opportunities, received 4,817 applications through the Grants.gov Web site, and paid $414,422.

Table 1. NEH and HUD Fiscal Year 2011 Grants.gov Contribution Amounts by Calculation Component

Agency	Agency size (% of contribution prior to caps)	Number of grants posted (% of contribution prior to caps)	Number of applications submitted (% of contribution prior to caps)	Total fiscal year 2011 contribution prior to the application of caps	Final fiscal year 2011 contribution after the application of caps
NEH	$50,000 (20%)	$69,298 (28%)	$131,933 (53%)	$251,231	$155,159
HUD	$200,000 (49%)	$65,998 (16%)	$139,205 (34%)	$405,203	$414,422

Source: GAO analysis of HHS data.

Note: The contribution calculation caps the year-over-year increase in contribution amounts for agencies classified as extra small and small to 20 percent. Component contribution amounts do not add up to the final contribution amounts due to the application of these caps on small and extra small agency contributions.

However, the National Endowment for the Humanities (categorized as a small agency for the purposes of Grants.gov) posted 42 grant opportunities, received 4,577 applications through the Web site, and paid $155,159. As shown in table 1, the majority of this difference is due to the agency size component of the funding calculation. NEH's agency size component is $50,000; HUD's is $200,000.

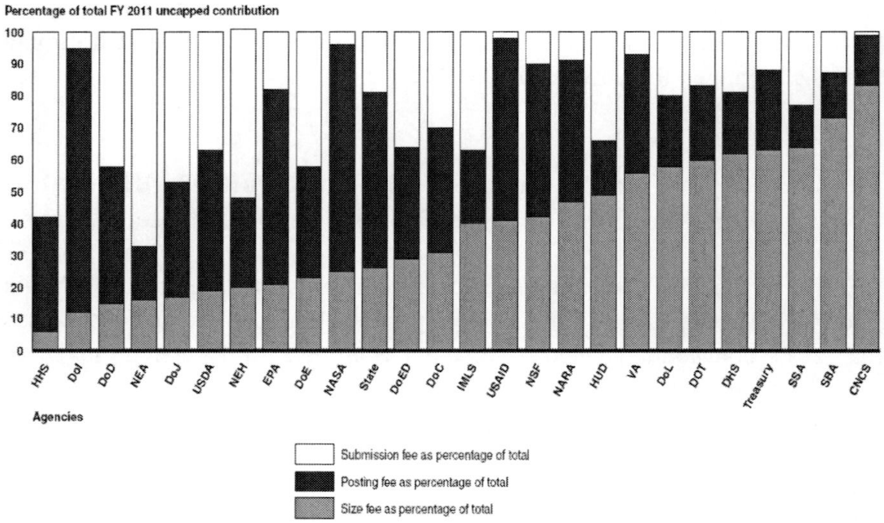

Source: GAO Analysis of HHS data.

Note: Analysis based on fiscal year 2011 agency contribution amounts prior to the application of the fiscal year 2011 caps. The 26 agencies in fig. 3 are the: Department of Health and Human Services (HHS), Department of the Interior (DoI), Department of Defense (DoD), National Endowment for the Arts (NEA), Department of Justice (DoJ), United States Department of Agriculture (USDA), National Endowment for the Humanities (NEH), Environmental Protection Agency (EPA), Department of Energy (DoE), National Aeronautics and Space Administration (NASA), Department of State (State), Department of Education (DoED), Department of Commerce (DoC), Institute of Museum and Library Services (IMLS), United States Agency for International Development (USAID), National Science Foundation (NSF), National Archives and Records Administration (NARA), Department of Housing and Urban Development (HUD), Department of Veterans Affairs (VA), Department of Labor (DoL), Department of Transportation (DOT), Department of Homeland Security (DHS), Department of the Treasury (Treasury), Social Security Administration (SSA), Small Business Administration (SBA), and Corporation for National and Community Service (CNCS).

Figure 3. Components of Agency Contribution as a Percentage of Fiscal Year 2011 Total Budget.

According to the GEB, the agency size factor is one of three factors used as a proxy for total agency Grants.gov system utilization. The GEB stated that gauging actual system use would require a longitudinal analysis of factors, including opportunities posted, applications submitted, and applications received. HHS and PMO officials told us that they consider agency size to correlate with an agency's use of the Grants.gov system; however, we found only a moderate correlation between partner agencies' use of the Grants.gov Web site (as defined by the Grants.gov contribution calculation) and agency size. When we analyzed fiscal year 2011 Grants.gov data for agency size, grants posted, and applications submitted, we found no clear pattern of increased system usage as agency size increased. While the average number of grants posted and applications accepted was the lowest for extra small agencies and highest for HHS (the only extra large agency), the relationship was inconsistent for small, medium, and large agencies. That is, some medium agencies have higher usage rates—under both measures—than some large agencies.

Further, for some agencies, agency size—the measure with the weakest link to system use—is the largest driver of an agency's contribution. As noted above, while charges based on the agency size component comprise only 20 percent of the total Grants.gov budget, they are often a larger or smaller percentage of a particular agency's contribution to Grants.gov. As shown in figure 3, 8 of the 26 partner agencies paid more due to their size than for Web site usage costs in fiscal year 2011.[11] Overall, partner agencies' payments based on size as a percentage of their total fiscal year 2011 contribution ranged from 6 percent for HHS to 83 percent for Corporation for National and Community Service (CNCS).

According to federal cost accounting standards, agencies should assign costs as closely as possible based on the amount of services or goods provided.[12] These standards list an order of preference for three cost assignment methods that should be used: (1) direct tracing of costs wherever economically feasible, (2) assigning costs on a cause-and-effect basis, or (3) allocating costs on a reasonable and consistent basis when not economically feasible to assign costs directly or on a cause-and-effect basis. Further, to the extent that agencies receive goods and services from HHS under the Economy Act, the amount paid must be based on the actual cost of goods or services provided.[13] The Economy Act is the authority cited by most agencies as the legal basis for transferring funds to HHS for Grants.gov services. In 2008, we reported that better allocation of system costs among users also promotes efficiency and perceived equity.[14] We said that requiring a beneficiary to pay for the services they receive promotes economic efficiency and that fees not based on use may result in under- or overcharging for services received and results in cross-subsidization between system users.

Grants.gov Does Not Track and Report on Certain Key Costs and Does Not Charge Agencies for All Known Costs

The Grants.gov PMO tracks costs for internal management purposes to ensure contract compliance and that program activities stay within GEB approved funding levels; however, it does not report costs by key program activities to its partner agencies, and it does not track or report on costs attributable to each partner agency. For example, the Grants.gov PMO updates GEB members at bimonthly board meetings with spending information on contracted activities and staff salaries but, according to HHS, detailed spending information by program activity or agency-specific requests are not provided. Absent this information, partner agencies' ability to link the services they received to their Grants.gov payments is limited, and the Grants.gov PMO cannot easily justify proposed increases to the Grants.gov budget or explain how changes in agency contributions—either stemming from changes in the contribution calculation or the total budget amount—align with services agencies will receive. One partner agency said that the inability to link services received to their Grants.gov payments causes delays in processing the Grants.gov MOU because the agency's MOU approval procedures require a documented link between costs incurred and payments made. The Grants.gov PMO told us that if asked to do so, they could track activity costs in greater detail, but that they are not set up to track costs by agency.

The type of cost tracking in our case study initiatives varied. For example, the Benefits.gov PMO prepares a strategic plan for partner agencies that links activities to system goals and costs. According to the Benefits.gov PMO, this type of reporting gives partner agencies the information to decide what system activities they would have to curtail to achieve lower payments. Integrated Acquisition Environment (IAE) officials we spoke with said that in addition to tracking costs by each of the eight systems they manage, they also provide annual reports describing the services partner agencies receive as well as the cost savings they realize through their participation in the IAE systems. None of the initiatives we spoke with, however, track costs by agency.

Further, although Grants.gov tracks the costs of providing on-line grant application forms to partner agencies for internal management purposes, it does not charge partner agencies commensurate with their use of these forms. Grant application packages can include multiple custom or standard on-line grant application forms, which the PMO creates and maintains at the request of partner agencies. According to the Grants.gov PMO, the cost of developing and maintaining these forms is increasing. Development of each custom form creates additional cost for the PMO, and Grants.gov incurs maintenance costs (e.g., license fees) for all active forms. Currently, each partner agency is allowed two new forms each year. However, some partner agencies request and receive more than two forms per year; others request new forms but also request that the old forms remain active. Since partner agencies' payments do not change based on their form usage, partner agencies that request fewer than two new forms each year subsidize agencies that request more than two forms. The PMO reports that the increasing cost of forms puts pressure on its ability to deliver other required services. The PMO said that it would like to include a measure of form activity in the contribution calculation, so that partner agencies with more form activity pay a higher share of system costs. The PMO has discussed this informally with members of the GEB but has not made a proposal to capture forms activity in the contribution calculation.

Lastly, because the Grants.gov contribution calculation does not account for all of Grants.gov's activity costs, it is unclear whether the weights assigned to the three measures in the contribution calculation actually represent the relative cost of each activity. For example, as mentioned above, the measure for posting grant opportunities accounts for 40 percent of the Grants.gov budget in the contribution calculation; however, the cost data necessary to make this linkage is not tracked or reported. Consequently, we found little evidence that the PMO spends 40 percent of its resources related to posting activities.

Grants.gov PMO Lacks Effective Strategies to Manage Known, Recurring Collection Delays

Grants.gov continues to receive the bulk of its funding late in the fiscal year. As we have previously reported, this has adversely affected Grants.gov operations. As shown in figure 4, Grants.gov received the majority of its fiscal year 2009 and fiscal year 2010 agency contributions 7 to 9 months into the fiscal year. In addition, HHS and OMB have cited delayed funding as a management risk to Grants.gov.[15] In 2009, according to the PMO, delayed funding nearly resulted in Grants.gov suspending operations. As we have previously reported, this funding pattern is not unusual for Grants.gov specifically or for legacy E-Gov initiatives in general.[16]

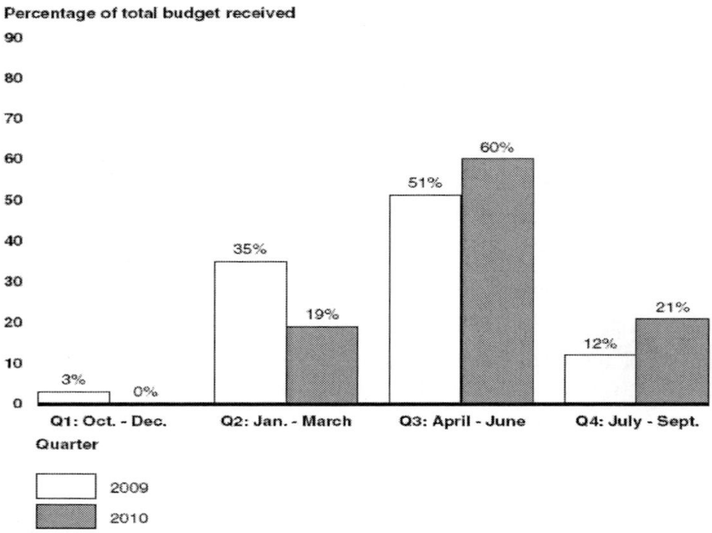

Source: GAO Analysis of HHS data.

Figure 4. Grants.gov Collection Timing, Fiscal Year 2009 and Fiscal Year 2010.

The Grants.gov PMO reported that collection delays complicate its ability to manage Grants.gov efficiently. Until it receives its contributions, Grants.gov is generally not permitted to expend funds for system maintenance, upgrades, or any other activities or purchases.[17] HHS and PMO officials said that to date, they have met all federal standards for executing contracts and eventually are able to obligate all partner agency contributions each fiscal year, but face difficulties, especially with small but crucial contracts, that are restricted by acquisition rules from crossing fiscal years. For example, the PMO said that for the first several months of fiscal year 2010, it was difficult and expensive to make changes to the Web site because the contract option period for the contractor who supported those changes had ended and there were no funds available to exercise the next option period. This resulted in many Web pages becoming outdated and required approximately 90 changes to Web pages when funds became available and support was restored.

Various factors contribute to funding delays. According to OMB, reasons for late or nonpayment of partner agency funds include internal agency issues and statutory requirements governing agencies' transfer of funds for E-Gov initiatives.[18] Additionally, the Grants.gov PMO and officials from other legacy E-Gov initiatives we interviewed reported that the process of managing the MOUs—which are the vehicles that lay out the amount and timing of contributions to be made in support of these E-Gov initiatives— is time consuming and contributes to funding delays. For example, both the Disaster Assistance Improvement Program (DAIP) and Benefits.gov PMOs noted that delays in collections from partner agencies posed a serious threat to their respective systems and all three case study managing partners stated that the enforcement of these agreements is costly to the PMOs. Managing recurring risks is a multistep process that includes evaluating and selecting risk management alternatives.[19] As we have previously reported, OMB staff recognize the risks the PMO faces in compelling agencies to pay on time, but said that with proper management such risks can be greatly mitigated. They added that other E-Gov initiatives face similar challenges but still run successful systems with higher levels of customer satisfaction, such as Business Gateway (www.business.gov) and Benefits.gov (www.benefits).

The E-Gov initiatives in our review use various strategies to manage collection delays. For example, all of them—including Grants.gov— prepare and distribute agency MOUs early in the fiscal year to facilitate rapid collection, as well as time contracts to begin mid or late in the fiscal year rather than at the start of the fiscal year. However, the IAE and DAIP PMOs report that two additional strategies are also useful in managing delays. They are: (1) depositing partner fees/contributions into multiyear appropriation accounts and (2) receiving some form of funds from their managing partners until partner agency contributions become available.

- *Multiyear Appropriation Accounts*. Integrated Acquisition Environment (IAE) and DAIP deposit their multiyear or no-year partner agency contributions into multiyear accounts. This allows the agency to carry over unobligated funds from one year to the next, which can help with cash flow issues during the early part of the fiscal year before current year funds become available. The IAE PMO reports depositing partner agency contributions into a revolving fund, and said that in previous years it was able to use unobligated funds (i.e., carryover) in the revolving fund to mitigate the adverse impact of receiving contributions later in the fiscal year. The DAIP PMO uses a different type of account—a multiyear, reimbursable account—to achieve the same outcome.[20]

- *Timing of Managing Partner Contributions.* Both IAE and DAIP have the benefit of receiving funds from their managing partner to tide them over between the beginning of a fiscal year and the point at which partner agency contributions are made available. The IAE PMO reports being able to borrow funds from GSA prior to receiving its partner agency contributions; it reimburses GSA once it receives its partner agency contributions. DAIP receives their managing partner's contribution in advance of the OMB E-Gov Benefits report issuance[21]— in January of fiscal year 2010 for example—which eases cash flow issues caused by receiving partner agency contributions late in the fiscal year.[22]

Grants.gov's contributions are deposited into an annual appropriation account. The PMO treats all contributions, including contributions from agencies that pay with multi- or no-year funds as being available for obligation only in the fiscal year of the contribution. That is, because the contributions are deposited into an account that closes at the end of each fiscal year, the Grants.gov PMO either obligates all of these funds by the end of each fiscal year, or returns them. Our review of available agency agreements found that 7 partner agencies in fiscal year 2008 and 10 partner agencies in fiscal year 2009 reported contributing multiyear or no-year funds to Grants.gov. These funds accounted for at least 20 percent of the Grants.gov budget in both years.[23] To create a more reliable funding stream for Grants.gov, PMO and HHS officials said that they are exploring several alternatives to the current system, including the use of revolving funds, multiyear reimbursable accounts, and direct appropriations. They are also exploring the possibility of keeping the funds in an annual appropriation account but having partner agencies delay transferring their no- or multiyear funds until the first quarter of the following fiscal year; these funds would be available in the fiscal year following the year for which the contribution was made. To date, HHS has not implemented these or other alternatives.

Experiences and lessons learned from other similar legacy E-Gov initiatives could help inform Grants.gov's deliberations as it considers options for addressing its funding-related challenges. HHS acknowledges the value in sharing information and met with the National Science Foundation, which serves as managing partner for the Grants Management Line of Business initiative in December 2010. The purpose of the meeting was to discuss Grants.gov's funding challenges and to explore potential funding alternatives. HHS also reported attending an April 2010 Grants/Acquisition Community collaboration meeting which included GSA IAE managing partner officials. Part of the purpose of the meeting was to discuss governance and IT funding of E-Government projects. However, HHS does not regularly meet with its counterparts in other legacy E-Gov initiatives. We have previously reported on the benefits of knowledge-sharing in a variety of government programs.[24] OMB encourages legacy E-Gov initiatives to share good practices, such as strategies used to manage collection delays, and has referred HHS to other E-Gov initiatives to seek guidance on this issue. Other E-Gov managing partners have also noted the benefits of such collaboration. For example, the DAIP and Benefits.gov PMOs have a long-standing collaborative relationship that, according to DAIP officials, includes sharing best practice information and lessons learned. In addition, DAIP officials noted that members of one of its governance bodies, typically representatives of other E-Gov offices, often share best practices from other E-Gov initiatives with which they have experience.

Recent Proposal to Merge Integrated Acquisition Environment and Grants.gov Does Not Address Funding Issues

The President requested $38 million for GSA in fiscal year 2012 to modernize and upgrade IAE operations. Of this amount, $500,000 would support the inclusion of Grants.gov functionality in a consolidation of GSA's Federal Business Opportunities (an IAE system that publicizes contract opportunities) and Grants.gov into a single Web site for both grant and contract opportunities, tentatively called Federal Opportunities; however, the proposal does not include a funding mechanism for operation and maintenance costs once the system is developed.[25] GSA currently expects the development of Federal Opportunities to be completed in fiscal year 2013.

Accountability and Responsibility for Grants.gov Performance among the Grants.gov Governance Entities Remains Unclear

Grants.gov continues to experience persistent governance challenges, including unclear roles and responsibilities among the governance entities, a lack of key performance metrics, and communication with stakeholders. Since we first reported on these issues in July 2009, some progress has been made in these areas. As previously discussed, although OMB and HHS have taken some steps to implement our recommendations to (1) develop and review performance metrics related to system availability, usability, and data integrity; and (2) develop guidance that defines roles and responsibilities of various governance bodies and ensures that the Grants.gov budget and funding model adequately supports the package of IT services approved by HHS's OCIO, these recommendations have not been fully implemented. Given the number of entities with management and oversight responsibilities for Grants.gov, clear roles and responsibilities for each and coordination among these entities is critical. In addition, information on system performance and costs is necessary to clearly link the benefits partner agencies receive with the costs they pay and may foster partner agency support for Grants.gov.

Unclear Roles and Responsibilities

As we previously reported, the GEB and HHS's OCIO share responsibility for reviewing and approving major changes to, and funding for, the Grants.gov system. In October 2009, the PMO indicated that it was working with the HHS Chief Information Office to ensure full adherence to the HHS Capital Planning and Investment Control Process (CPIC); in December 2010, the PMO told us that Grants.gov is subject to all HHS IT Investment Control and Security policies appropriate to major IT investments. The PMO also described a closer working relationship with the OCIO and said that since early 2009, HHS executives in the Grants, Budget, and CIO offices have been regularly briefed on Grants.gov status. In addition, HHS as the managing partner of Grants.gov attends OCIO and IT Review Board meetings and communicates information back to the Grants.gov PMO. According to a PMO official, the GEB continues to provide IT capital planning governance. However, HHS officials also told us that there is a disconnect between system requirements and the funding to meet those requirements. As an example, HHS officials cited the GEB's historical inability to fund an adequate disaster recovery capability. In commenting on a draft of this report, HHS provided additional information on its CPIC process after we completed our work on this engagement, including a new IT acquisition approval process implemented as of February 24, 2011. The process applies to all IT acquisitions greater than $10,000—including Grants.gov— and includes an IT Acquisition Approval Checklist—which requires reporting the total cost of the acquisition. These new policies above make it more likely that Grants.gov will be reviewed through the CPIC process. However, until HHS's OCIO can demonstrate that it directly receives and reviews the GEB-approved budget for Grants.gov and approves Grants.gov activities based on the GEB-approved funding levels, HHS lacks assurance that Grants.gov's funding levels will support the functions approved through CPIC.

Key System Performance Measures

Since our July 2009 report, the Grants.gov PMO has made progress in developing improved system performance measures. In commenting on a draft of this report, an HHS official said that in December 2010 they launched an initiative to implement Foglight, a system performance monitoring tool. As part of this effort, HHS developed a draft set of performance metrics for service availability, system performance, and system usage, and is in the process of discussing the draft measures with its stakeholders to solicit input on potential performance metrics for the Grants.gov system. However, until HHS finalizes and deploys a set of well-designed performance measures it will continue to lack a clear picture of system performance and information about how well applicants are being served.[26] Further, as we previously reported, in response to the recurring difficulties with the Grants.gov system some agencies continue to accept applications through agency-specific electronic systems, by e-mail, or mail, under at least some circumstances.[27] Absent better information on the health of the Grants.gov system—and a means to use that information to improve system performance—partner agencies have little incentive to reduce their reliance on potentially duplicative agency-specific grant application systems.

Grants.gov's current strategic plan contains high-level statements on strategic vision, mission, and goals, but does not include specific performance goals or information on current and planned initiatives. HHS officials acknowledged that they should update their strategic plan; the Grants.gov PMO told us that it initiated planning activities during the first quarter of fiscal year 2011, such as developing a documented annual work plan, that would include proposed PMO activities for each quarter and its progress in completing those activities.

Communication with Partner Agencies

HHS provides partner agencies with feedback opportunities but does not communicate some key performance and cost information. In an effort to better inform partner agencies about Grants.gov operations, a PMO official said that the Grants.gov Agency User group meets monthly, and helps provide an open line of communication between the PMO and partner agencies. The PMO official noted that, as part of an effort to increase transparency and provide more substantive opportunities for two-way feedback between Grants.gov and partner agencies, HHS sponsored forums held in January and February 2010, attended by 21 of the 26 partners. During these sessions, HHS solicited feedback and provided updates on the status of past partner agency recommendations. The PMO also surveyed partner agencies about their priorities for new system requirements.

In spite of these efforts, Grants.gov partner agencies have expressed interest in obtaining more information on system performance and costs. For example, an official from one agency said that he would like to see more information about performance metrics for the Grants.gov Web site and call-in center and more transparency about program activity costs, such as agency-specific costs. The PMO does not routinely provide partner agencies with detailed spending plans or reports linking costs to activity, program goal, or agency-requested services because, as previously discussed, it generally does not track information in this way. Absent this information, agencies lack a clear picture of the benefits they receive from Grants.gov compared to the costs they pay, hampering their support of and satisfaction with Grants.gov. The PMO said that it does report on the costs and trade-offs of significant changes to system operations when significant realignments of program resources are required by statute, regulation, best practice, or when proposed by the GEB.

We have previously reported that agreeing on roles and responsibilities and developing mechanisms to monitor, evaluate, and report on results can help increase the success of interagency collaborative efforts such as Grants.gov.[28] By doing so, federal agencies can better address their partner agencies' expectations and gain their support in achieving joint objectives.

NEW FEDERAL GRANTS GOVERNANCE MODEL IS UNDER OMB REVIEW

In December 2009, the Grants Task Force, a group composed of representatives from the GEB and the GPC, including a representative from HHS, submitted a proposal for a Federal Grants Governance Framework to OMB. In February 2010, the Task Force met with OMB to further discuss the issue. As of April 2011, the proposal remains under OMB review. The framework describes a new governance body that would replace the GEB and the GPC. The new body would report directly to OMB and would serve as the federal grants advisory body responsible for establishing the direction for and coordinating all governmentwide grants initiatives, including Grants.gov. The framework calls for a single point of contact in OMB. A GPC official said that a single point of contact ("a champion for the grants community") in OMB would encourage decisiveness and clear communication. In addition to consolidating the GEB and GPC, the proposed framework would integrate the policy, IT, operations, and oversight functions of both bodies and includes an OMB representative as a co-chair or sponsor. The Grants.gov PMO would be represented on an operations committee. Finally, the proposed framework will foster involvement by the external grantee community and encourage collaboration between federal grant-making agencies as well as between those agencies and the public. OMB has not provided a time frame for finishing its review. We note that significant changes to the Grants.gov governance model are unlikely until OMB completes its review and announces a new Grants.gov governance framework.

As a preliminary, high-level concept document, it is understandable that the proposal does not flesh out details as to how the framework would be implemented, but it lacks even a high-level overview of several critical elements. For example, while the proposal appears to clarify the roles of the GEB and PMO, and provide structure for their interaction it does not address the role of the managing partner CIO—a critical entity in managing the Grants.gov system as an IT system—nor the relationship between the CIO and the new governance bodies. Importantly, the proposed governance framework does not appear to address the challenges that emerge when different entities are responsible for approving system funding and system requirements, as is currently the case with Grants.gov.

CONCLUSIONS

The Grants.gov system has faced funding and governance challenges that have adversely affected Grants.gov operations. HHS and OMB have worked diligently to manage and mitigate these issues in the short run. However, concerns about Grants.gov's funding calculation and governance persist, and some partner agencies also maintain their own, potentially duplicative grants management systems—contrary to the streamlining and cost-saving intent behind Grants.gov and the federal grants streamlining legislation on which it is based. OMB and the Grants.gov governance entities continue to consider longer-term improvements to Grants.gov— such as potentially consolidating the separate grants and contracts application systems and implementing a new advisory body for governmentwide grants initiatives. While we recognize that the Grants.gov PMO's ability to address governance issues is somewhat limited until OMB completes its review of the proposed governance framework, we believe that the time is ripe to reconsider whether a number of factors—the package of activity costs charged to users, how those costs are distributed among users, and the PMO's strategies for managing persistent collection delays—will help or hinder Public Law 106-107's goals of simplifying and streamlining grant administration. It is also an opportune time for Grants.gov to consider whether there are lessons to be learned from similar legacy E-Gov systems that could inform improvements in these areas.

Grants.gov has taken steps to move closer to a fee-for-service funding model. However, three significant issues remain. First, the current method of distributing costs among partner agencies results in agencies that use Grants.gov to similar degrees paying vastly different amounts for service; second, the contribution calculation does not account for the development and maintenance of grant application forms—a reportedly growing cost for the PMO. Third, the Grants.gov PMO does not report costs by key program activities to its partner agencies, and it does not track or report on costs attributable to each partner agency. As such, agencies' payments for Grants.gov's services may be misaligned with the costs they impose on the system. The importance of analyzing and understanding system costs is not limited to Grants.gov; it will also be a critical issue for GSA's Federal Opportunities system so that GSA, partner agencies, and Congress have the best possible information available to them when considering how— and at what level—to fund the new system. Absent a well-designed funding mechanism, Federal Opportunities runs the risk of the same kind of funding challenges currently facing Grants.gov.

Grants.gov continues to suffer from untimely agency contributions and the PMO continues to report this issue as a serious threat to its continuing operations. This issue is not unique to Grants.gov. However, while Grants.gov and other E-Gov managing partners employ some of the same risk management strategies to mitigate the effects of delayed funding, some take mitigating steps by: (1) depositing partner fees/contributions into multiyear appropriation accounts and (2) receiving funds from their managing partners before partner agency contributions are made available for use. We believe that, to the extent that they are available to Grants.gov, these strategies could significantly improve Grants.gov's cash flow and allow for more efficient operations in the earlier part of each fiscal year.

Although a proposal to restructure federal grants management systems remains under OMB review we believe that HHS can take interim steps to address immediate Grants.gov governance and performance issues. Although HHS has taken important steps to gather information on potential performance measures, more needs to be done. Grants.gov's performance measures remain in draft form; the Grants.gov strategic plan does not include specific performance goals and information on current or planned initiatives, and the Grants.gov PMO does not communicate key system performance information to partner agencies. Absent full implementation of these initiatives information gaps about the health of the Grants.gov system will persist. However, collecting performance information is not enough; unless this information is made available to stakeholders and used to inform decision making, the Grants.gov governance entities will lack a valuable management tool for developing strategies to better achieve results.

Lastly, we continue to believe in the value of knowledge-sharing between Grants.gov and similar legacy E-Gov initiatives. Discussing and modifying for its own use the experiences and lessons learned from similar legacy E-Gov initiatives—such as DAIP, Benefits.gov, and IAE—could help inform Grants.gov's deliberations as it considers how to best address its funding- and management-related challenges.

Recommendations for Executive Action

We are making the following four recommendations to the Secretary of Health and Human Services to improve economic efficiency and support effective management of the Grants.gov system:

- HHS should work with the Grants Executive Board—or similar organization should the governance structure change—to improve the allocation of costs among users by developing and implementing a calculation that more clearly links agency contributions to their system use.
- HHS should build on and use its existing cost-tracking capabilities to expand its cost information and communicate that information to partner agencies in greater detail. This includes capturing, charging for, and reporting on all Grants.gov services provided to partner agencies.
- HHS should link its strategic plan to an annual operating plan that links costs and spending to performance goals and milestones, and includes progress against goals and system initiatives.
- HHS should build on its recent outreach efforts and engage in knowledge sharing with the managing partners of other E-Gov initiatives.

AGENCY COMMENTS & OUR EVALUATION

We provided a draft of this report to the Secretary of Health and Human Services and the Director of the Office of Management and Budget. OMB staff provided us oral technical comments that were incorporated as appropriate.

In written comments, the HHS Assistant Secretary for Legislation concurred with our overall findings and recommendations. HHS's written comments are reprinted in appendix V. Key comments include that HHS "is proud of the significant progress made since the government-wide "Boost" to enhance system capacity, performance, and ensure the public has reliable access to a central portal to find and apply for federal assistance opportunities." HHS also stated that "long term strategic planning as well as short term operations including acquisition activities ... are hampered by the uncertainties associated with the level of funding and schedule of funding availability" and "if a "Fee for Service" model is not adopted and Grants.gov remains tied to the E-Gov Benefit Report, HHS recommends federal grant policy be changed to require OMB transmit the E-Gov Benefits report to Congress by December 1st." In regards to governance issues, HHS "appreciates the work of the Grants Governance Taskforce in supporting the Grants.gov PMO and recommending governance changes, and hopes that

OMB will soon make its final determination on the federal grants governance framework." We agree that delayed funding poses a serious risk to Grants.gov's operations. As stated earlier in this report, HHS and OMB have both cited delayed funding as a management risk to Grants.gov. We said that, given the timing of when the E-Government report is typically issued, funds are generally not available for transfer until near the beginning of the third quarter of each fiscal year. We believe that adopting a fee-for-service model would go a long way toward addressing Grants.gov's funding issues. We also agree, as stated in this report, that significant changes to the Grants.gov governance model are unlikely until OMB completes its review. In addition, HHS provided updated information, technical comments, and suggested edits that were incorporated where appropriate.

We are sending copies of this report to the Secretaries of Health and Human Services, Homeland Security, and Labor; the FEMA and GSA Administrators; the Director of the Office of Management and Budget and to appropriate congressional committees. The report also is available at no charge on the GAO Web site at http://www.gao.gov.

If you or your staff members have any questions or wish to discuss the material in this report further, please contact me at (202) 512-6806 or czerwinskis@gao.gov. Contact points for our Offices of Congressional Relations and Public Affairs may be found on the last page of this report. GAO staff who made key contributions to this report are listed in appendix VI.

Stanley J. Czerwinski
Director
Strategic Issues

APPENDIX I: OBJECTIVES, SCOPE, AND METHODOLOGY

To examine the Grants.gov system and make recommendations to improve system management, we evaluated (1) key factors the Department of Health and Human Services (HHS) should consider when proposing a funding model for Grants.gov and (2) how the Grants.gov governance bodies could address Grants.gov's previously identified governance challenges. To address both objectives, we gathered and reviewed reports and documentary evidence from the Office of Management and Budget (OMB), the Grants.gov Program Management Office (PMO), and the Grants Executive Board (GEB). We also conducted interviews with relevant officials from OMB, HHS, and the GEB.

We also reviewed relevant legal authorities and guidance as well as previous GAO work on Grants.gov, E-Government (E-Gov) initiatives, federal user fees, and interagency collaboration. In addition, we analyzed Grants.gov funding data to determine the relationship between agency use of the system and payments. Specifically, we analyzed the relationship between the agency size designation and other measures of system use.

To obtain additional information for both objectives, we conducted case study reviews of three agencies that are managing partners of other E-Gov initiatives: the Department of Labor (DOL), managing partner of Benefits.gov; the Department of Homeland Security (DHS), managing partner of Disaster Assistance Improvement Program (DAIP); and the General Services Administration (GSA), managing partner of Integrated Acquisition Environment (IAE). To make the case study selections, we collected data from HHS on the partner agencies of Grants.gov and from OMB on the governance and funding models used by all legacy E-Gov initiatives. We selected a nongeneralizable sample including DHS, DOL, and the Department of the Interior (DOI) as case study agencies because they fulfilled our criteria of being (1) managing partners to legacy E-Gov initiatives with funding and governance models similar to Grants.gov and (2) partner agencies of the Grants.gov system. As the engagement progressed, we substituted GSA for DOI as a third case study E-Gov initiative because Grants.gov officials identified GSA as managing a complex, similar E-Gov system (IAE) and because GSA recently piloted an electronic grants system at OMB's request. These case studies are not representative of all E-Gov initiatives or partner agencies of Grants.gov. To draw on the experiences of other managing partners of E-Gov initiatives, we reviewed available reports and documentary evidence and conducted interviews at all case study agencies. In order to obtain more information from the perspective of partner agencies of Grants.gov, we reviewed documentation and interviewed relevant officials at DHS, DOL, and DOI.

We assessed the reliability of the data we used for this review by interviewing knowledgeable agency officials, reviewing related documentation, and reviewing the data for outliers and missing data. Based on our review, we determined the data were sufficiently reliable for our purposes. We conducted this performance audit from April 2010 to May 2011 in accordance with generally accepted government auditing standards. Those standards require that we plan and perform the audit to obtain sufficient, appropriate evidence to provide a reasonable basis for our findings and conclusions based on our audit objectives. We believe that the evidence obtained provides a reasonable basis for our findings and conclusions based on our audit objectives.

APPENDIX II: BENEFITS.GOV

Purpose: To provide citizens with a single point of entry to government benefit and assistance programs.

Managing partner agency: Department of Labor (DOL)

Number of partner agencies (including managing partner): 17

Fiscal year (FY) 2011 expected agency contribution total: $3,557,033

Table 2. Benefits.gov Expected Agency Contributions for Fiscal Year 2011

Agency	FY 2011 contribution
Department of Commerce	$69,201
Department of Education	$259,753
Department of Energy	$205,596
Department of Health and Human Services	$326,948
Department of Homeland Security	$164,477
Department of Housing and Urban Development	$293,852
Department of the Interior	$122,355
Department of Justice	$51,148
Department of Labor	$725,824
Department of State	$83,241
Department of Transportation	$110,320
Department of the Treasury	$175,509
Department of Veterans Affairs	$200,582
Small Business Administration	$225,654
Social Security Administration	$256,744
U.S. Department of Agriculture	$285,829
Total	$3,557,033

Source: GAO presentation of DOL data.

Note: Partner agencies that do not make financial contributions are not included in this table.

Funding: According to the Program Management Office (PMO), Benefits.gov uses a fee-for-service funding model.

Each agency's contribution is calculated using four measures of system usage. The four measures and their weights are as follows:

- the number of partner agency programs posted (weight= 1.0),
- page views by public (weight= 4.5),
- Benefits.gov traffic outbound to the agency (weight= 3.5), and
- agency traffic inbound from agency to Benefits.gov (weight= .50).

Partner agencies are ranked based on their usage of each of the four measures. This ranking is multiplied by the weight for that metric. The result is the number of shares an agency has in the program. The inbound traffic measure—when internet users click on links at an agency's Web site to connect to Benefits.gov—is designed to be an incentive. More inbound traffic from a particular agency reduces that agency's contributions. The total approved budget for a fiscal year is divided by the total number of partner shares. The resulting share price is then multiplied by each partner agency's number of shares, thus resulting in an agency funding level for that fiscal year. DOL, the managing partner, pays more than the contribution calculation would call for to reflect its responsibility for the system.

Governance: The Benefits.gov governance model is as follows:

- Benefits.gov Program Management Office (PMO): Day-to-day operations are performed by the PMO. The PMO is responsible for activities such as keeping the site running and updated, paying the program's vendors, and updating the Benefits.gov governance bodies.
- Benefits.gov Change Control Board (CCB): The CCB is comprised of representatives from each of the 17 partner agencies. Representatives vet all proposals that are developed by the CCB or the PMO before they go to the Governance Board. The CCB also oversees development of the annual strategic and performance plans. The CCB meets four times per year.
- Working Groups: Working Groups are formed by members of the CCB and other federal partner agency subject matter experts to deal with a specific issue as it arises. Working Groups meet as needed.
- Governance Board: The Governance Board is comprised of Chief Information Officers (CIOs), or their designees, from each partner

agency and provides ongoing strategic guidance to the program manager. These individuals represent their agency and vote on all funding and governance decisions. The Governance Board meets four times per year.

APPENDIX III: DISASTER ASSISTANCE IMPROVEMENT PROGRAM (DAIP)

Purpose: To provide a single portal where citizens can identify forms of federal disaster assistance that may be relevant through a prescreening questionnaire, apply for disaster assistance using a single application, and check the status of their application requests.

Managing partner agency: Department of Homeland Security (DHS)/Federal Emergency Management Agency (FEMA)

Number of partner agencies (including managing partner): 17

Fiscal year (FY) 2011 expected agency contribution total: $18,400,000

Funding: According to the DAIP Program Management Office (PMO), DAIP has adopted a new funding model for fiscal year 2012 that contains elements of an agency contribution and a transaction-based (fee-forservice) model. Under the fiscal year 2012 model, DHS/FEMA will contribute 94 percent of the total DAIP budget. The remaining 6 percent will be divided among the contributory partner agencies based on five measures of system usage. The five measures and their relative weights in the calculation are:

- the number of times data are exchanged between an agency interface and disasterassistance.gov (weight = -30),
- the number of times each agency's forms of assistance are identified as applicable to their situation by a registered disaster survivor (weight = -20),
- the number of times each agency's forms of assistance are viewed (weight = 50),
- the number of transfers from disasterassistance.gov to an agency Web site (weight = 40), and
- the number of transfers from an agency Web site to diasasterassistance.gov (weight = 30).

Table 3. Disaster Assistance Improvement Program Expected Agency Contributions for Fiscal Years 2011 and 2012

Agency	FY 2011 contributions	FY 2012 contributions
Department of Commerce	$30,000	$12,337
Department of Defense	-	-
Department of Education	$84,333	$49,349
Department of the Interior	$41,241	$41,124
Department of Justice	$95,949	$50,378
Department of Labor	$410,708	$115,149
Department of Health and Human Services	$194,124	$133,655
Department of Homeland Security	$15,846,838	$17,388,337
Department of Housing and Urban Development	$129,999	$111,036
Department of State	-	$12,337
Department of Transportation	-	-
Department of the Treasury	$129,299	$116,177
Department of Veterans Affairs	$193,749	$47,293
Small Business Administration	$464,667	$94,586
Social Security Administration	$182,508	$64,771
U.S. Department of Agriculture	$555,344	$133,655
U.S. Office of Personnel Management	$41,241	$29,815
Total	$18,400,000	$18,400,000

Source: GAO presentation of DHS data.

The weights for two measures are negative, reducing partner agencies' contributions. Negative weights act as incentives to partner agencies to perform these activities. Partner agencies receive a ranking based on their usage under each metric. This ranking is multiplied by the weight for that metric. The result is the number of shares an agency has in the program. The total approved budget for a fiscal year is divided by the total number of partner shares. The resulting share price is then multiplied by each partner agency's number of shares, thus resulting in an agency funding level for that fiscal year.

Governance: The DAIP governance model is as follows:

- DAIP Program Management Office (PMO): The PMO handles day-to-day operations such as keeping the site running and updated, and paying the program's vendors.
- Working Group: The Working Group is chaired by the DAIP program manager and consists of representatives assigned by their agencies. This group includes two types of partners, voting partners (those who provide monetary support of the program) and advisory partners (those who attend meetings to advise the group on topics within the agency area of expertise). The Working Group provides direction to the DAIP PMO regarding the execution of the program strategic plan and scope and provides recommendations to the Executive Steering Committee for ratification decisions on all major program initiatives. The Working Group meets biweekly.
- Working Group Subcommittees: Subcommittees are made up of volunteers from the Working Group. Subcommittees have been used for developing the program strategic plan, scope, funding model, performance measurement, and lessons learned procedures.
- Executive Steering Committee: This committee consists of appointees from each federal partner agency. This group includes voting and advisory partners. Voting partners ratify all decisions related to funding and strategy. The committee meets quarterly.

APPENDIX IV: INTEGRATED ACQUISITION ENVIRONMENT (IAE) INITIATIVE

Purpose: To integrate and streamline the federal procurement process through electronic means. IAE consists of eight systems under one organizational umbrella.

Managing partner agency: General Services Administration (GSA)
Number of partner agencies (including managing partner): 24
Fiscal year (FY) 2011 expected agency contribution total: $40,574,591

Table 4. Integrated Acquisition Environment Initiative Expected Agency Contributions for Fiscal Year 2011

Agency	FY 2011 contributions
Department of Commerce	$194,889
Department of Defense	$26,373,484
Department of Education	$54,656
Department of Energy	$1,957,912
Department of Health and Human Services	$1,635,490
Department of Homeland Security	$1,668,346
Department of Housing and Urban Development	$39,180
Department of the Interior	$299,160
Department of Justice	$712,563
Department of Labor	$145,153
Department of State	$719,638
Department of Transportation	$359,001
Department of the Treasury	$358,606
Department of Veterans Affairs	$1,747,180
Environmental Protection Agency	$108,139
General Services Administration	$1,483,007
National Aeronautics and Space Administration	$1,783,828
National Science Foundation	$15,067
Nuclear Regulatory Commission	$6,964
Small Business Administration	$2,872
Social Security Administration	$39,124
U.S. Agency for International Development	$131,734
U.S. Department of Agriculture	$615,145
U.S. Office of Personnel Management	$123,453
Total	**$40,574,591**

Source: GAO presentation of GSA data.

In addition to the IAE Initiative, the IAE program also receives funding through the IAE-Loans and Grants initiative. The IAE-Loans and Grants initiative funds the expanded use of the Data Universal Numbering System that assigns a unique identifier to all recipients of federal awards as required by the Federal Funding Accountability and Transparency Act and the American Recovery and Reinvestment Act. In fiscal year 2008, OMB directed the IAE Program Management Office (PMO), which is responsible for overseeing the Data Universal Numbering System, to issue Memoranda of Agreement to 22 partner agencies to cover the cost of this expanded service. Fees for the IAE-Loans and Grants initiative are calculated using a different funding calculation than the IAE initiative described in this report and annually add $6.5 million to the total IAE program budget.

Funding

According to the PMO, IAE uses a fee-for-service funding model. IAE uses a funding calculation to determine the fees of the 24 partner agencies. Initially, two partner agency measures are used: (1) the annual obligated dollar volume of contracts and (2) the annual number of transactions. A "transaction" is defined as any modification, new contract, or other action which would require the use of an IAE system. Both of these measures are provided by the Federal Procurement Data System (FPDS). Partner agencies are divided into three tiers based on the two measures. The FPDS data on dollar volume of contracts and number of transactions used to determine an agency's tier are from the most current completed fiscal year (i.e., data from fiscal year 2008 will be used in the fiscal year 2011 calculation). The funding calculation is updated each year. A weight is assigned to each tier (.01, .02, or .03).

This weight is multiplied by each agency's FPDS total dollar volume and the result is divided by 100 to determine each agency's weighted share of the budget. Each agency's weighted share is divided by the sum of all agencies' weighted shares (not including the Department of Defense's shares) to determine the agency percent of 35 percent of the total IAE initiative budget. The agency percent is multiplied by the total IAE initiative budget to get the agency's contribution. The Department of Defense—the largest agency user of the IAE system both in terms of dollar volume and number of transactions—pays 65 percent of the total IAE budget. This cap was agreed to in 2004 and is reviewed annually to determine if a cap is required.

Governance

The IAE governance model is as follows:

- The Program Management Office (PMO) is responsible for day-to-day program support. The PMO holds monthly meetings with the program managers of each of IAE's eight systems.
- The IAE Transition Planning Team Review Board is responsible for reviewing and approving changes to IAE operations and programs. The board is organized within the PMO and is composed of the individual system program managers. The board meets twice monthly.
- The Acquisition Committee for E-Gov is the executive steering committee that makes broad and long-term decisions regarding IAE. The committee's responsibilities include reviewing and voting on the IAE budget and funding models. The committee includes representatives of IAE partner agencies and OMB and meets monthly.
- In addition, the eight IAE systems have a consolidated Change Control Board that includes partner agency voting members. The consolidated CCB recommends and approves internal system changes. Individual system Project Managers are part of both the consolidated CCB and the IAE Transition Planning Team Review Board.

APPENDIX V: COMMENTS FROM THE DEPARTMENT OF HEALTH AND HUMAN SERVICES

DEPARTMENT OF HEALTH & HUMAN SERVICES

OFFICE OF THE SECRETARY

Assistant Secretary for Legislation
Washington, DC 20201

APR 26 2011

Stanley J. Czerwinski
Director, Strategic Issues
U.S. Government Accountability Office
441 G Street N.W.
Washington, DC 20548

Dear Mr. Czerwinski:

Attached are comments on the U.S. Government Accountability Office's (GAO) draft report entitled: "GRANTS.GOV: Additional Action Needed to Address Persistent Governance and Funding Challenges" (GAO 11-478).

The Department appreciates the opportunity to review this draft report prior to publication.

Sincerely,

Jim R. Esquea
Assistant Secretary for Legislation

GENERAL COMMENTS OF THE DEPARTMENT OF HEALTH AND HUMAN SERVICES (HHS) ON THE GOVERNMENT ACCOUNTABILITY OFFICE'S (GAO) DRAFT REPORT ENTITLED, "GRANTS.GOV: ADDITIONAL ACTION NEEDED TO ADDRESS PERSISTENT GOVERNANCE AND FUNDING CHALLENGES" (GAO-11-478)

The Department appreciates the opportunity to review and comment on this draft report. We concur with the report's overall findings and recommendations and offer the following comments:

Managing Partner Role & System Performance

HHS, as the largest grant making entity in the federal government, takes seriously its managing partner role of Grants.gov and is proud of the significant progress made since the government-wide "Boost" to enhance system capacity, performance and ensure the public has reliable access to a central portal to find and apply for federal assistance opportunities.

- Since the completed "Boost" activities in April 2010, the Grants.gov system has experienced only 2 unplanned outage as compared to *routine* user interruptions experienced in early 2009 and prior years.
- The Grants.gov website logged more than 11 million site visits in Fiscal Year (FY) 2010; and processes an average of over 250,000 applications per year.
- The system's processing speed is exceptional - validating prospective grantee applications in less than three minute compared to previous processing times which averaged five to ten minutes in length.
- Since 2009, Grants.gov has completed six technical builds to further enhance system functionality and improve users' experience including: the ability to export data into Excel, streamline workflow and access 24 hour user support. With the Grants.gov system fully stable, the Grants.gov Program Management Office (PMO) is working to complete implementation of additional performance monitoring metrics that will be meaningful to a wide array of stakeholders and will help to identify system issues.

As the managing partner, HHS ensures strong executive and managerial support for the Grants.gov system across the Department. HHS CIO is fully engaged in the Grants.gov PMO's capital planning efforts, IT investment considerations (including analytic support of the system's Exhibit 300), and security monitoring through the Department's Certification and Accreditation process.

Funding Model

The current Grants.gov funding model hampers the Grants.gov PMO's ability to meet its financial obligations and ensure continued system availability. Long term strategic planning as well as short term operations including routine acquisition activities (such as the timely procurement of updated software licenses) are hampered by the uncertainties associated with the level of funding and schedule of funding availability.

The current contribution-based funding model requires approval by the Grants Executive Board (GEB) and OMB concurrence (which is the driving factor) of the Grants.gov annual budget, and does not allow for the collection of funds until after OMB issues the ***Report to Congress on the Benefits of the President's E-Government Initiatives*** (E-Gov Benefit Report) in February or March.

GENERAL COMMENTS OF THE DEPARTMENT OF HEALTH AND HUMAN SERVICES (HHS) ON THE GOVERNMENT ACCOUNTABILITY OFFICE'S (GAO) DRAFT REPORT ENTITLED, "GRANTS.GOV: ADDITIONAL ACTION NEEDED TO ADDRESS PERSISTENT GOVERNANCE AND FUNDING CHALLENGES" (GAO-11-478)

In FYs 2009, 2010 and 2011, HHS, as managing partner, requested budgetary increases for Grants.gov to accommodate user requests for additional system functionality. All budget increase requests were denied by the GEB and OMB; the latter makes the formal decisions.

In both FYs 2010 and FY2011, delayed production & delivery of the E-Gov Benefits Report led to a lack of funds until almost the 3rd quarter of the fiscal year. Collection of funds is further delayed from some agencies due to their congressional requirement to reprogram funds from their respective appropriations committees; in FY2010, Grants.gov was still missing more than $370k in owed agency contributions as of September 16, 2010. This situation placed the Grants.gov program at risk for lapsing funds because standard acquisition processing timelines had passed.

Grants.gov is a fully operational system and is no longer considered a "new" systems development project. The E-Gov Benefits Report provision was constructed for new programs that had not yet made it to an operational status.

The outdated funding model, constraints associated with the program's ties to the E-Gov Benefits report, and delayed agency partner contributions place the program and the system at risk by forcing us to "pass the hat" in order to pay for our routine operations, maintenance and customer support activities

HHS requested in 2009 and 2010, that Grants.gov receive formal designation as a "mature" program and that mature programs be allowed to receive funding starting October 1st of the fiscal year. OMB has not approved these requests to change the system's designation.

A "Fee for Service" model that incorporates collection of funds for required operations and maintenance, legislative and policy modifications, and enhancements that keep the product in line with technology advances is also suggested. If a "Fee for Service" model is not adopted and Grants.gov remains tied to the E-Gov Benefit Report, HHS recommends federal grant policy be changed to require OMB transmit the E-Gov Benefits report to Congress by December 1st.

Governance

By design, the current governance structure overseeing Grants.gov places all members of the GEB with responsibility to:

> "provide oversight, executive sponsorship, Agency participation, and Agency resource contributions for the Grants.gov as well as Agency review and sponsorship for GMLOB. The Board will define accountability and reporting requirements to be met by the Program Management Offices. The Grants Executive Board will focus on the following areas of strategic interest:
> - Grants.gov implementation, operation, budgets and funding algorithms, funding, and foundations for long-term service." (GEB Charter, January 2007)

Even though HHS has the most thorough understanding of the Grants.gov program and system needs, in its role as Managing Partner (and as evidenced by HHS' funding requests in FYs 2009, 2010 and 2011)

GENERAL COMMENTS OF THE DEPARTMENT OF HEALTH AND HUMAN SERVICES (HHS) ON THE GOVERNMENT ACCOUNTABILITY OFFICE'S (GAO) DRAFT REPORT ENTITLED, "GRANTS.GOV: ADDITIONAL ACTION NEEDED TO ADDRESS PERSISTENT GOVERNANCE AND FUNDING CHALLENGES" (GAO-11-478)

it does not have the authority to adjust Grants.gov's programmatic budget without the agreement of 26 different constituents.

HHS appreciates the work of the Grants Governance Taskforce in supporting the Grants.gov PMO and recommending governance changes, and hopes that OMB will soon make its final determination on the federal grants governance structure.

End Notes

[1] http://www.grants

[2] GAO, *Recovery Act: Consistent Policies Needed to Ensure Equal Consideration of Grant Applications*, GAO-09-590R (Washington, D.C.: Apr. 29, 2009) and GAO, *Grants Management: Grants.gov Has Systemic Weaknesses That Require Attention*, GAO-09-589 (Washington, D.C.: July 15, 2009).

[3] Office of Management and Budget, *Recovery Act Implementation—Improving Grants.gov and Other Critical Systems*, M-09-14 (Washington, D.C.: Mar. 9, 2009) and Office of Management and Budget, *Improving Grants.gov*, M-09-17 (Washington, D.C.: Apr. 8, 2009). In April 2010, OMB reported that these risks had been successfully mitigated and instructed federal grant-making agencies to resume using the apply function of Grants.gov for all programs that previously used this functionality by April 30, 2010. See Office of Management and Budget, *Grants.gov - Return to Normal Operations*, M-10-16 (Washington, D.C.: Apr. 23, 2010). According to the Grants.gov PMO, all federal partners but one—with some additional individual programmatic exceptions—use both the find and apply functions. In fiscal year 2010, 4,217 discretionary synopses were posted and 246,631 applications were submitted.

[4] Pub. L. No. 106-107 (Nov. 20, 1999).

[5] For more information on Public Law 106-107 implementation, see GAO, *Grants Management: Additional Actions Needed to Streamline and Simplify Processes*, GAO-05-335 (Washington, D.C.: Apr. 18, 2005), GAO, *Grants Management: Grantees' Concerns with Efforts to Streamline and Simplify Processes*, GAO-06-566 (Washington, D.C.: July 28, 2006) and GAO-09-589.

[6] Office of Management and Budget, *E-Government Strategy* (Washington, D.C.: Feb. 27, 2002).

[7] Pub. L. No. 107-347 (Dec. 17, 2002).

[8] Office of Management and Budget, *FY 2004 Grants.gov Funding and Advance Planning Guidance for FY 2005-FY 2006*, M-04-14 (Washington, D.C.: June 18, 2004).

[9] Prior to fiscal year 2010, agency size was the sole basis for determining agency contributions.

[10] The fiscal year 2010 and fiscal year 2011 contribution calculations are the same and use fiscal year 2007 data to measure Web site usage. The GEB approved the use of fiscal year 2008 data to calculate the Web site usage measures in the fiscal year 2012 contribution calculation. In all other aspects the fiscal year 2012 contribution calculation is the same as the one used in fiscal year 2010 and fiscal year 2011.

[11] These agencies are: (1) CNCS, (2) SBA, (3) SSA, (4) Treasury, (5) DHS, (6) DOT, (7) DoL, and (8) VA.

[12] Statement of Federal Financial Accounting Standards (SFFAS) No.4, Managerial Cost Accounting, Concepts and Standards for the Federal Government (July 31, 1995).

[13] 31 U.S.C § 1535(b).

[14] GAO, *Federal User Fees: A Design Guide*, GAO-08-386SP (Washington, D.C.: May 29, 2008).

[15] Office of Management and Budget, *Improving Grants.gov*, M-09-17 (Washington, D.C.: Apr. 8, 2009).

[16] For example, in 2005, we reported that most of the 10 legacy E-Government initiatives that were funded by agency contributions experienced shortfalls from their funding plans for fiscal years 2003 and 2004; in most cases contributions from partner agencies were made in the third and fourth quarters of those fiscal years. In 2009, we reported that such delays

persisted for Grants.gov, with 37 percent of their fiscal year 2009 partner contributions being paid by March 2009 and 88 percent paid by the end of June 2009.

[17] HHS, as the managing partner, provides the Grants.gov PMO funds to pay staff salaries and benefits as well as to maintain their physical offices from the beginning of the fiscal year until Grants.gov receives its partner agency contributions. The only exceptions are tasks performed by contractors under contracts funded with prior fiscal year funds with performance periods extending into the current fiscal year.

[18] For example, since fiscal year 2006 agencies may not make funds available for transfers or reimbursements to OMB's E-Government initiatives until 15 days after OMB submits an E-Government report to the House and Senate appropriations committees and until the committees approve the transfer of these funds. *See e.g.,* Consolidated Appropriations Act, 2010, Pub. L. No. 111-117, div. C, title VII, § 733 123 Stat. 3213. In fiscal year 2010, this report was issued on March 5, 2010—a time frame that OMB officials described as consistent with previous years. Given the timing of when the E-Government report is typically issued, funds are generally not available for transfer until near the beginning of the third quarter of each fiscal year. In fiscal year 2011, the report was issued on February 17, 2011. Further, some agencies also have specific limitations on their agency contributions to E-Government initiatives, such as reprogramming/notification requirements.

[19] The GAO Risk Management Framework divides risk management into five major phases: (1) setting strategic goals and objectives, and determining constraints; (2) assessing risks; (3) evaluating alternatives for addressing these risks; (4) selecting the appropriate alternatives; and (5) implementing the alternatives and monitoring the progress made and results achieved. See *Risk Management: Further Refinements Needed to Assess Risks and Prioritize Protective Measures at Ports and Other Critical Infrastructure*, GAO-06-91 (Washington, D.C.: Dec. 15, 2005).

[20] In all cases, the ability to legally carry forward unobligated balances is subject to the funds' period of availability. That is, the funds contributed must be legally available for obligation beyond the fiscal year. Unless otherwise specifically provided for, amounts contributed do not automatically assume the time character of the account or fund to which they are transferred. See 31 U.S.C. § 1532; B-319349, June 4, 2010.

[21] The DAIP PMO also reports that it is seeking full managing partner funding for disasterassistance.gov. DAIP PMO staff view this move as important to reducing the disruption of late agency payments and the staff time involved in MOU review and enforcement. In fiscal year 2011, DHS is expected to pay 86 percent of DAIP's budget. In 2010, the DHS OIG recommended full DHS/FEMA funding of DAIP to stabilize the funding model; however, this recommendation has not been implemented (see Department of Homeland Security Office of the Inspector General, *FEMA's Disaster Assistance Improvement Plan*, OIG-10-98, June 2010).

[22] Not every partner contribution constitutes a transfer of funds, which is defined as a shifting of all or part of the budget authority in one appropriation or fund account to another. See *A Glossary of Terms Used in the Federal Budget Process*, GAO-05-734SP (Washington, D.C.: September 2005), at 95.

[23] Our review of Grants.gov MOUs included all 26 partner agency MOUs for fiscal year 2008 and MOUs for 25 of the 26 partner agencies for fiscal year 2009. In each year, some of the MOUs did not specify the type of funds (one-year, multiyear or no-year). For that reason, we can state that at least 20 percent of funds were multi- or no-year funds.

[24] GAO, *Information Sharing: Federal Agencies Are Sharing Border and Terrorism Information with Local and Tribal Law Enforcement Agencies, but Additional Efforts Are Needed*,

GAO-10-41 (Washington, D.C.: Dec. 18, 2009); GAO, *Older Driver Safety: Knowledge Sharing Should Help States Prepare for Increase in Older Driver Population*, GAO-07-413 (Washington, D.C.: Apr. 11, 2007).

[25] The consolidated system is based on a "proof of concept" pilot conducted in 2009-2010. OMB directed GSA to initiate the pilot so that lessons learned could inform OMB's efforts to modernize the broader federal grants structure, including how these systems interact with agencies' own grants and contracting systems.

[26] Grants.gov's only performance measures that address system performance are tied to customer satisfaction.

[27] GAO-09-589.

[28] GAO, *Results-Oriented Government: Practices That Can Help Enhance and Sustain Collaboration among Federal Agencies*, GAO-06-15 (Washington, D.C.: Oct. 21, 2005). The eight key practices are as follows: define and articulate a common outcome; establish mutually reinforcing or joint strategies; identify and address needs by leveraging resources; agree on roles and responsibilities; establish compatible policies, procedures, and other means to operate across agency boundaries; develop mechanisms to monitor, evaluate, and report on results; reinforce agency accountability for collaborative efforts through agency plans and reports; and reinforce individual accountability for collaborative efforts through performance management systems. Two of the eight factors are identified in this report as lacking in Grants.gov's collaborative efforts with its partner agencies.

In: Federal Grant Management
Editor: Vanessa N. Rowley

ISBN: 978-1-62100-185-0

Chapter 7

IMPROVING THE GRANT MANAGEMENT PROCESS*

United States Department of Justice, Office of the Inspector General

The Office of the Inspector General (OIG) Audit Division conducts internal audits of Department of Justice (D0J) granting agencies and external audits of grant recipients.[1] Internal audits assess overall grant program management in areas such as awarding grants, monitoring grantees, and assessing program performance and reporting. External audits assess a grantee's compliance with grant conditions, including budget management and control, drawdown and reimbursement requests, program income, subgrantee oversight, matching funds, financial reporting, and program reporting.

Since its inception in April 1989, the OIG's Audit Division has conducted over 30 internal audits of the Office of Justice Programs, the Office of Community Oriented Policing Services, and the Office on Violence Against Women. The OIG Audit Division has conducted almost 900 external audits of grant recipients, and the Audit Division has also assisted the OIG Investigations Division on grant related investigations.

---

* This is an edited, reformatted and augmented version of the United States Department of Justice, Office of the Inspector General publication, dated February 2009.

1 Throughout this document, the term granting agencies refers to the Office of Justice Programs, the Office of Community Oriented Policing Services, and the Office on Violence Against Women.

The OIG's Investigations Division investigates allegations of fraud related to DOJ-funded grant programs. These investigations have led to criminal convictions, civil recoveries, administrative recovery of funds, and debarments of individuals and grantees. Additionally, the Investigations Division provides proactive "Grant Fraud Awareness" training to granting agency personnel and external audiences to increase awareness of grant fraud issues.

Based on the OIG's 20 years of work in these areas, we developed the following list of ideas and practices that granting agencies should consider adopting to minimize opportunities for waste, fraud, and abuse in awarding and overseeing the $4 billion in DO] funding contained in the American Recovery and Reinvestment Act of 2009. This list includes practices that could be implemented in the short term (within 30 days), the medium term (within 1 year), and the long term (over 1 year).

Grant Program Development

The initial stage of any grant program is the most important. If a program is not well developed, it is difficult to adequately implement or monitor it. To form a sound foundation, grant programs should have clear and strong objectives prior to soliciting applications. Further, it is essential that all participants in the grant program share a common understanding of the program purpose. Participants often have different interpretations, which prevents a federal strategy from being implemented.

- Program objectives therefore need to be developed in a timely manner to focus the efforts of all participants and to clarify expectations. To prevent the appearance that the program does not a have focused direction, grantees must not receive funding prior to submitting an application or before overall program objectives are established.
- With each program solicitation, measurable and obtainable performance measures should be established to ensure that legislative intent and program objectives are met.

GRANT APPLICATIONS

- While some applicants are experienced grantees with sophisticated grant writers, others may have never applied for a DOJ award. To ensure that all applicants are able to submit an application within the required timeframe, DOJ should establish and publicize an Internet site where grantees or potential grantees can submit questions and receive answers within 1 business day, and a telephone hotline to speak with a grant advisor.
- Granting agencies should set up or expand on-line opportunities for s-training for grantees, such as tutorials on grant do's and don'ts.
- The application process could be used to identify potential "red flags" for granting agencies to follow-up on prior to making awards. The application could include questions such as: (1) will funds be deposited in a separate account, (2) do you have written accounting procedures, (3) do you have an inventory system in place, (4) do you have an accounting system that can separately track all drawdowns and grant expenditures, (5) what performance measures have you established to determine if the grant objectives are being met, (6) what data will you collect to measure your progress in meeting performance measures, (7) do you have a management risk assessment process in place to identify and mitigate potential risks, and (8) what is your records retention policy?
- Audits often find that grantees do not maintain timesheet documentation for personnel costs. The application process should include verification that timesheets for all personnel are maintained to document hours worked for grant and non-grant-related activities.
- Granting agencies should enhance pre-award screening to ensure that only applications that meet solicitation objectives and requirements are sent to peer reviewers.
- Granting agencies should establish criteria to gauge the risk associated with new grantees. For new grantees assessed to be high risk, grantee agencies should conduct background checks to verify proper payment of withholding taxes, credit standing, and other indicators of problems. In addition, grantee agencies should conduct Internet searches or other reference checks to identify negative information that should be considered prior to granting an award. For example, good sources of information include the General Services Administration's Excluded Parties List System, U.S. Attorneys, the

Drug Enforcement Administration, the Federal Bureau of Investigation, the U.S. Marshals Service, the Bureau of Prisons, and other granting agencies.

- Granting agencies should review open OIG Audit and Inspections reports to determine whether grantee progress in implementing corrective action is sufficient to award additional grants.
- Granting agencies should check to make sure no ongoing OIG or other criminal investigations are in process before deciding to make awards.

Award Process

- Granting agencies should clearly document key aspects of the award process and maintain this documentation, such as the: (1) basis for noncompetitive awards, (2) peer reviewers' agreement with the peer review consensus report, (3) basis for award selections that differ from peer review or program manager recommendations, and (4) procedures used to identify and remedy conflicts of interest among agency staff and external experts involved in the peer review process.
- To decrease the risk of unknowingly awarding funds to a high-risk grantee, a DOJ-wide procedure should be established that allows granting agencies to share information on high-risk grantees prior to awarding funds.
- Granting agencies should consider mandating that high-risk grantees maintain separate bank accounts for grant funds, including separate accounts for each grant. This would make the use of grant funds more transparent and reduce the grantees' ability to hide improper use of grant funds.
- Granting agencies should determine a grantee's progress on
- implementing the requirements of prior grants before awarding additional grants for identical purposes.
- Granting agencies should include information on fraud awareness in grantee award packages.
- In the single audits, we are seeing an increase of the number of municipalities that have been formally designated as a "distressed municipality" by their respective states and are essentially in receivership with regard to financial management. These grantees may need federal grant funds, but they should automatically be

designated high-risk and monitored more closely to ensure funds are accounted for and appropriately spent.

MONITORING

- Granting agencies should fully utilize an effective risk assessment model so they can provide proper monitoring. The risk assessment should include "red flag" indicators so that granting agencies can provide on-site assistance or on-site reviews to grantees with risk factors. Examples of "red flag" indicators include: inadequate separation of cash-related duties, inadequate internal controls, inadequate financial management system, prior grant mis-management, and prior fraud.
- Granting agencies should increase their monitoring of grantees and subgrantees by increasing site visits and reviewing financial and progress reports for accuracy, completeness, and alignment with project goals. This practice is particularly important for new grantees, as well as for experienced grantees with problems managing prior grants.
- Granting agencies should conduct site visits earlier in the grant period to catch potential problems. As part of the site visits, they should ensure that the grantee is maintaining accurate accounting records and adequate support for its expenditures.
- Granting agencies should require more specificity in grantee reporting. For example, a granting agency can require a report showing budgeted amounts versus expenditures by line item so that a reviewer can see how the funds are being spent. This will reinforce the requirement that the grantee should be adhering to the proposed budget.
- For grantees designated as high-risk, grant managers should periodically require the submission of supporting documentation so reported expenditures and achievements can be verified.
- Granting agencies should ensure the state administering agencies engage in and report back to the granting agencies on their specific monitoring and oversight of subgrants. This is often overlooked and is a major weakness in the process.
- To increase transparency, granting agencies should require state agencies to make subgrant award documents readily available to the

public. This will increase the number of people who may detect potential problems and make subrecipients more likely to follow award guidelines.

- Granting agencies should have a process to ensure that all instances of alleged misuse of grant funds are properly documented and reported to the proper agency authorities and the OIG for appropriate and timely follow-up and resolution.
- Granting agencies should strengthen procedures for referring problem grantees, along with specific detailed information regarding the problems, to the OIG for audit or investigation.
- Granting agencies should require grantees to display OIG hotline posters in common areas to ensure proper referrals of fraud issues to the OIG.
- As required by the initial implementing guidance issued by the Office of Management and Budget for the Recovery Act, granting agencies should include a requirement that each grantee or sub-grantee awarded funds made available under the Recovery Act shall promptly refer to the OIG any credible evidence that a principal, employee, agent, contractor, sub-grantee, subcontractor, or other person has submitted a false claim under the False Claims Act or has committed a criminal or civil violation of laws pertaining to fraud, conflict of interest, bribery, gratuity, or similar misconduct involving those funds. In addition, and beyond what is required by the OMB guidance, granting agencies also should require the grantee or sub-grantee when they become aware of an overpayment of funds distributed to the grantee or sub-grantee to promptly report to the OIG and granting agency that overpayment.
- For grantees with the potential to have significant problems, granting agencies should maximize the use of special conditions, such as requiring: (1) third-party management of grant funds, so that all expenditures and drawdowns are authorized and completed by a third party that has no vested interest in the grantee; (2) authorization to proceed with the next phase of a project based upon evidence of acceptable performance; and (3) more detailed financial reports.
- Grantee agencies should establish early intervention teams to make site visits to high-risk grantees within 30 days of grant awards.
- Granting agencies should consider seeking supporting documentation from all grantees for randomly selected drawdown requests of

Financial Status Reports to ensure that these figures are supported by logical and verifiable financial transactions.

- Granting agencies should review and modify existing internal policies and guidance so that it is clear that their personnel are required to report anomalies or other indicators of the misuse of grant funds to the DIG and internal agency offices for appropriate follow-up.

PERFORMANCE

- Granting agencies need to establish a better policy for determining when to allow retroactive approval for violations of requirements and conditions versus requiring the grantee to repay questioned costs. Generally, granting agencies now provide a retroactive approval or waive questioned costs and therefore encourage non-compliance by grantees.
- Granting agencies should assist grantees in determining the appropriate information to collect in order to assess program performance. (The Office of Justice Programs recently incorporated this in its measures for the Byrne Grant program.) Progress reports submitted to granting agencies often include program outputs, such as the number of people served, rather than measures that assess whether the program is achieving its intended objective. Granting agencies should develop this type of guidance for each of their grant programs.
- Granting agencies should have procedures in place to ensure that all decisions made in response to grantee requests are documented in writing. Grantees often state that the granting agency provided verbal approval for a particular course of action. When there is no documentation to support the grantee's statement, the auditors must disallow the use of grant funds in that situation.
- Granting agencies should ensure they have a process to carefully review grantee's narrative progress reports to ensure the program is successfully meeting its stated objectives and to identify grantees that are at a high risk of failing to fulfill their stated goals and mission.

TRAINING

- Key grantee officials (such as the person submitting Financial Status Reports) should be required to take annual grant administration training that covers financial and programmatic requirements, and fraud awareness. This could be implemented via an on-line training program that can administer a test to ensure the recipient understands the basic requirements and can track the recipient's completion of the training.
- Granting agencies should offer annual training to their grant administrators to reinforce administrative, financial, and programmatic requirements for the types of grants they award. This training should include grant fraud awareness and risk assessment training to remind participants of the specific risks to these funds, encourage discussion of fraud prevention and detection techniques, and emphasize employees' obligations when they identify indicators of misuse or fraud.
- Granting agencies should provide opportunities for the grant administrators to discuss common questions and problem areas grantees experienced to ensure consistent treatment by the granting agencies. These feedback and discussion sessions could be a good tool for developing the topics for training that key grantee officials will take on an annual basis.

COMMUNICATIONS

- Granting agencies need to increase communication with their grantees, and in particular, new grantees. A common complaint from grantees is that the granting agency's program managers are either non-responsive or not available to answer questions.
- To facilitate communication with and among grantees, granting agencies should expand the use of communication tools such as Really Simple Syndication (RSS) feeds, blogs, and wiki applications hosted on the granting agencies website.
- Granting agencies should reach out to state audit agencies that provide coverage of grantee management and solicit both coverage of and feedback on grantees' use of D03 funds.

Additional Considerations – Impact on Granting Agencies Financial Statements and Information Systems

- Granting agencies' Chief Financial Officers should consider the effect that new grants and grant spending programs will have on their agency's grant accrual estimate methodology. Specifically, the Chief Financial Officers should evaluate the Recovery Act grants separately to see if they are being reported, drawn down, or spent differently than other grants.
- Granting agencies' Chief Information Officers should develop procedures to alleviate the strain on their agency's information systems (specifically the financial reporting systems) from the massive number of applications, drawdowns, and SF-269 submissions that will occur within in a short period after the Recovery Act grants become available.

INDEX

A

B

C

T

U

V

W